THE WORLD'S EPOCH-MAKERS

DAVID HUME
and
His Influence on Philosophy and Theology

THE WORLD'S EPOCH-MAKERS

DAVID HUME
and
His Influence on Philosophy and Theology

by

James Orr, M.A., D.D.

Professor of Apologetics and Systematic Theology

United Free Church College, Glasgow

GYAN

Published by

GYAN

Gyan Publishing House
5, Ansari Road
Daryaganj, New Delhi-110002
Phone: 011-47034999, 9811692060
E-mail: books@gyanbooks.com

Distribution Network
gyanbooks.com
India, USA, Canada, UK, Australia, France

ISBN : 978-81-212-2297-6 (PB)
First Published, 1903

2nd Impression 2021

Printed at: Gyan Press, Delhi.

David Hume
and
His Influence on Philosophy and Theology
Author: James Orr

THE WORLD'S EPOCH-MAKERS

David Hume and His Influence on Philosophy and Theology

By

James Orr, M.A., D.D.

Professor of Apologetics and Systematic Theology
United Free Church College, Glasgow

Edinburgh. T. & T. Clark

1903

PREFACE

THE present sketch of the life, philosophy, and influence of Hume is based on well-nigh a lifetime's familiarity with the works of that author; but is, the writer feels, still very imperfect. It is only necessary in this Preface to specify sources of information, with the editions of Hume's Works referred to in the text, or that may profitably be consulted, and briefly to indicate one or two principles that have been followed in the composition of the book.

For the Life of Hume the main authority must always be Dr. J. Hill Burton's elaborate work, the *Life and Correspondence of David Hume*, supplemented by Dr. G. Birkbeck Hill's *Letters of David Hume to William Strahan*, with the full and valuable notes in that volume. With both will naturally be compared the brief sketch, entitled *My Own Life*, which Hume himself wrote shortly before his death, with a view to its being prefixed to future editions of his works. The ease of style, naïveté, and candour of self-revelation of the life-motives of its author, invest this autobiographical piece with more than usual interest. For the outer and anecdotal side of Hume's Edinburgh life, with sketches of his contemporaries, and of the society in which he and they moved, the reader may be referred to "Jupiter" Carlyle's *Autobiography*, and to the recent works of the Rev. H. G. Graham on *Social Life in Scotland*, and *Scottish Men of Letters*, in the eighteenth century. The spirit in these will be found entirely sympathetic.

The references in the text to Hume's works are to that edition which the writer has been longest acquainted with, and has mainly used—the old four-volume edition of Hume's Philosophical Works, published by Messrs. A. & C. Black in 1854. It was his intention to adjust the references to the excellent later edition of Hume's Works by T. H. Green and T. H. Grose; but in the end he found that certain advantages attached to the method originally adopted, and accordingly adhered to it. The peculiar value of Green and Grose's edition, it need hardly be said, lies in Prof. Green's exhaustive examination of Hume's *Treatise* in his Introduction to that work, and in the "History of the Editions," prefixed to the *Essays* by Mr. Grose. More recently, fresh proof has been given of the interest in Hume by the publication by the Clarendon Press of careful reprints of Hume's *Treatise* and his two *Enquiries*, edited with admirable Introductions, comparative tables, and full analytical indices, by Mr. L. A. Selby-Bigge, M.A. Mention should also be made of Leslie Stephen's *English Thought in the Eighteenth Century*. With these aids, and the more popular works of Huxley, Knight, and Calderwood, the student should be at no loss to get at the true "inwardness" of Hume's philosophy. This little work can only be offered as a further humble contribution, from its own point of view, to the same end.

The edition of the *History* to which references are made is (unless otherwise specified) the final edition, embracing the author's "last corrections and improvements." The edition is in eight volumes, and the special issue used is that of 1796.

It is indicated in the text that the point of view from which Hume's philosophy is mainly regarded is that of an experiment to explain knowledge, and generally the intellectual and moral outfit of man, without the assumption of a rational nature in man. The criticism in the volume, on the other hand, is directed to show (1) that the processes of Hume which ignore the rational self—the operation of reason—in the building up of a theory of knowledge, are invalid; and (2) that the rational self—the assumption of a rational thinking principle in man—alone solves the problems he raises. Hume is treated in this endeavour to solve the problem of knowledge without rational presuppositions as a type. It is astonishing to those familiar with his thought to find how much of it is present in, and continues in varying forms to be reproduced by, popular empirical philosophy. Origin of knowledge in vivid and faint states of consciousness; the potency of association; the "I" as a flowing stream of consciousness; no substantive self; no objectively existing world; no freedom; good as pleasure and evil as pain; utility the standard of morals; dismissal of rational Theism, and "natural histories" of religion; with much else that will readily occur to the observer of present-day tendencies.

In dealing with this widespread and prolonged influence of Hume, some method had to be adopted. It was impossible to deal with *all* ramifications of that influence, and the simplest principle seemed to be to keep in view mainly certain representative authors and schools. Kant has been chosen as representing the critical-rational standpoint — the more that he acknowledges his direct awakening by Hume; Reid and Hamilton (in part Brown) represent the Scottish school; J. S. Mill and Mr. Bain are selected as prominent Associationalists; Mr. Spencer stands for himself; Wundt and Prof. W. James are taken as types of the physiological psychology of the newer period. Mr. J. S. Mill is called upon also to do duty for utilitarianism in morals. Mr. Green may be held to represent idealism. It is impossible that in so brief a sketch even scant justice should be done to all these phases of thought, but there is at least the consistent endeavour to do none of them *in*justice. Such as the book is, it must now further speak for itself.

The thanks of the writer are due to the Rev. J. M. Wilson, B.D., London, for his kind assistance in correction of the proofs.

CONTENTS

DAVID HUME

CHAPTER I

INTRODUCTORY

DAVID HUME justly takes rank as the most distinguished member of that brilliant circle of literary men whose names gave such a lustre to the second half of the eighteenth century in Scotland. His speculations were the most profound, and, with the possible exception of Adam Smith in a particular department, his influence was the widest and most deeply felt, of any. Hume's contemporaries could hardly be expected to do him justice. His daring subtleties and avowed scepticism excited so many prejudices, and exposed him to so much dislike, that only a few were able and prepared to recognise his substantial merits. But even his warmest friends could scarcely have predicted the influence he was destined to exercise, or the important results that were to spring from his thoughts. It required time to clear away the mists that had gathered round his name, and to place him in his true light in the eyes of posterity. At a century and a half's distance, we are in a better position to take an impartial survey of his work and its effects. The result must be, that, however we may judge of Hume in particular respects, we cannot deny to him a right to the title of a great and independent thinker. It will be recognised that he arose at the proper time to accomplish a necessary task. He excited thought; he awoke men from their "dogmatic slumbers"; he gave an impulse to fresh speculation on the most important questions; by exploding old systems, he prepared the way for new. The study of such a man and his work can only be for our advantage. It is the purpose of this volume, after sketching his career, to describe the character, and endeavour to appraise the value, of the services he has directly or indirectly performed in the different directions of his influence.

It is not necessary at this preliminary stage to say much of Hume himself, though the man and his philosophy are in good measure of a piece, and must always be studied together. Hume's character, happily, is not one which it is difficult to sum up. Of easy, passionless disposition, good-tempered and kindly of heart, with little interest in outward nature, but much in the springs of human thought and action, with barely a spark of ideality in his composition, and, as one is compelled to judge, almost wholly without experience of the religious sentiment, he had yet, within the limits which such a nature imposes, a keen, subtle, and observant mind in the various branches of speculative inquiry, and a firm and settled purpose to work out for himself a reputation as an original discoverer in philosophy and morals. It is not unfair to speak, as is here done, of religion as an element almost entirely lacking in Hume's nature. We can at least find no unambiguous trace of it in anything he ever said, or did, or wrote. He seems to have early convinced himself that the bases of the ordinary religious beliefs, even those of the current Deism, were vanity, and that the philosopher would spend his time better in sceptically explaining, or explaining away, these beliefs, than in allowing them any influence over his own conduct. He has himself told us[1] that his ruling passion was "love of literary fame"; but, combined with this, he had a stubborn independence of nature, a praiseworthy desire to excel in what was best, and a courage and perseverance, that bore him easily through rebuffs and difficulties. He never lost his faith that, whatever the immediate judgment might be upon his work, his reputation was safe with posterity; and in this particular, at least, his confidence has been justified. His place in the world of thought and letters is assured beyond all possibility of altering it.

The influences which moulded the mind of Hume were partly Scotch, partly English, and in considerable measure French. With respect to Scotland, it must be acknowledged that Hume did far more to arouse the reflective spirit, and encourage the literary taste, of his countrymen, than they ever did to develop his. Till Francis Hutcheson—an Irishman—began, by his lectures in Glasgow, to attract attention to Scotland as a seat of the higher learning,[2] our country had but a poor reputation in that regard. Her literature was

[1] *My Own Life*; cf. below, p. 18.

[2] Dugald Stewart dates the rise of Scotland's metaphysical philosophy, and indeed of her literary taste in general, from the period of Hutcheson's lectures about 1729. But this lack of culture in Scotland may easily be exaggerated, and often has been. See below on the Scottish gentry, p. 15.

scanty; her scholarship, except in theology, associated mainly with one illustrious name—that of Buchanan. The reaction which, after the middle of the century, raised Edinburgh to a pinnacle of distinction in letters, was yet in its infancy when Hume began to write. Nevertheless, his admiration for Hutcheson, and the close intimacy which he afterwards maintained with most of the literary characters of the metropolis, must have exercised not a little influence on his later style. To England his debt was greater, though his rooted dislike to the English people prevented him from ever fully acknowledging it. His own strong ambition from the first was to gain distinction as an elegant writer of the English language, and this naturally led him to the study of the best models. A large share of his attention, in republishing his works, was always given to weeding out any lingering "Scotticisms" from their pages. His own estimate of the state of literature in England was far from high. "The first polite prose we have," he tells us in one of his Essays, "was writ by a man who is still alive" (Dean Swift).[1] Philosophy, except in the department of ethics, was, in his judgment, at an even lower ebb.[2] Men's minds had sunk to sleep under the influence of Locke. Vigorous, original thinking in regard to fundamental questions there was practically none. The Essay form of literature, which had risen into prominence, represented an attempt to unite thoughtful and instructive reading with the charm of a free and popular style; in this way it diffused important moral lessons and helped to elevate the public taste. Such compositions, especially

[1] "Of Civil Liberty" (Works, iii. p. 98).

[2] See Introduction to the *Treatise*.

after the failure of his first great work to attract attention, Hume seems to have looked on as models of an "easy and humane" philosophy, and to have kept them before him in the preparation of his books. But his deepest impressions were probably those which he derived from France. It was there that he composed his *Treatise of Human Nature,* and during his whole life his relations with France and with French authors were very intimate. The easy, pleasure-loving temper of that light-hearted people appears always to have possessed a singular fascination for his mind. He eulogises them repeatedly as models of what "sensible, polite, and knowing" people ought to be.[1] He caught the tone of their principal writers; he adopted many of their views of life; he made it the aim of his philosophy to justify their views by reasoning away every notion which could give life a higher meaning; he lowered his moral standard to a level almost exactly suited to their practice. The contrast of French life and manners to the narrow, intolerant spirit he found prevailing in certain circles in his own country (though all earnestness was apt to be harshly judged by him), may have helped to create a deeper sympathy in his mind with the former.

One feature of Hume's character requiring to be kept in view in all estimates of his work and aims is that already mentioned—his prevailing ambition to excel in literature. It was, he does not conceal, his "ruling passion" to take a permanent and brilliant place in the world of "polite letters." It is no disparagement of Hume to say that this predominant literary ambition was not

[1] See *My Own Life,* and the panegyric in the Essay above quoted (Works, iii. pp. 97–8); and cf. below, pp. 64,

favourable to the highest development of his powers as a thinker. There is a limit beyond which a man cannot go in philosophy without being content to sacrifice many of the graces of composition which are essential to purely literary success. Abstruse thinking will never bring in large returns of immediate popularity. To think or write like an Aristotle, a Kant, or a Hegel, is certainly not the road to literary fame such as Hume was in search of. And Hume was latterly, at least, perfectly aware of this. He contrasts the "easy and obvious philosophy" of popular writers, with "the abstruse philosophy" of deeper thinkers—which had also been his own earlier and nobler ideal[1]—and remarks, "It is certain that the easy and obvious philosophy will always, with the generality of mankind, have the preference over the accurate and abstruse. . . . This also must be confessed, that the most durable, as well as the justest fame, has been acquired by the easy philosophy. . . . The fame of Cicero flourishes at present, but that of Aristotle is utterly decayed."[2] In these circumstances, as a man bent on "the most durable as well as justest fame,' Hume has scarcely an alternative. He must either resign altogether the pursuit of the abstruser philosophy, or at least so modify and popularise it, that it will not debar him from taking his place among the "easy" writers. This, in fact, is what he proposes to attempt. "The difficulty," he says, "may perhaps be surmounted by care and art. . . . Happy if we can unite the boundaries of the different species of philosophy, by reconciling profound inquiry with clearness, and truth with

[1] Introduction to *Treatise* (Works, i. p. 6); see below, p. 32.

[2] In *Enquiry* (Works, iv. pp. 2, 3).

novelty."[1] It is easy to see that a thinker with such aims is committed to a style of writing in which more durable qualities are apt to be sacrificed to a desire to please.[2] It is a significant commentary on Hume's judgment, that it is the unfortunate *Treatise*, which he was fain to disavow because of its abstruseness, on which his fame as a philosopher now securely rests; while the more polished version of his principles in the *Enquiry* is relegated to a quite secondary place.

The purely literary merit of Hume's writings is, nevertheless, very great. He bestowed the utmost pains on the acquirement of an easy, fascinating style, and, once it was acquired, he lost no opportunity of polishing and perfecting it. His success in this latter endeavour may be almost regarded as complete. His style combines the greater number of those excellences of diction and smooth arrangement, for the study of which the eighteenth century was distinguished beyond most periods of our literature. It wants the "pomp and strut" of the style of Gibbon; it is less artificial than Robertson's; it unites the ease and grace of Addison with a peculiar clearness derived from his French favourites. It was a style admirably suited to the acute and flexible mind of the man who used it.

[1] Works, iv. p. 14. In a letter late in life he expresses the wish that he had always confined himself to "the more easy parts of erudition" (Burton's *Life*, i. p. 98).

[2] Professor Huxley also remarks: "Indeed, it appears to be by no means improbable that this peculiarity of Hume's constitution was the cause of his gradually forsaking philosophical studies, after the publication of the third part (on Morals) of the *Treatise*, in 1740, and turning to those political and historical topics which were likely to yield, and did in fact yield, a much better return of that sort of success his soul loved. . . . Verily he had his reward, but not the crown he might have won" (*Hume*, pp. 11, 12).

It served him to equal purpose in the literary essay, in the subtle analysis of mental phenomena, in the close train of metaphysical reasoning, and in the connected exposition of historical events and sequences. If it has any special fault, it may be said to lie in a certain lack of concentration and vigour, and in the absence of anything resembling passion. This is, perhaps, scarcely a defect in treating of subjects of a purely speculative nature, where the *lumen siccum* is a condition of success; but it is different in the study of history and of religion, where sympathy and the power of appreciating spiritual forces are indispensable qualifications. Still, as a master of correct and pleasing composition, Hume will always hold an honourable place among the great writers of our language. Dugald Stewart traces much of the elegance observable in the style of some of Hume's opponents to the careful and minute study which their desire to refute his views caused them to bestow upon his works,[1] and there can be no question that his influence in this respect has been both great and beneficial.

Of the contemporaries of Hume, the two who stand next to him in the measure of their importance are undoubtedly Adam Smith and Thomas Reid. The one is the acknowledged founder of political economy as a distinct branch of knowledge; the other is the recognised head of the Scottish School in philosophy. But even as regards these distinguished men, a pre-eminence must be assigned to Hume; for apart from his influence probably neither of the two would have written as he did. To Hume, as we shall find, more

[1] *Dissertation*, p. 208.

than to any living man, Adam Smith was indebted for the leading ideas of his principal work; and from Hume, as best understanding the completeness and value of the exposition, the *Wealth of Nations* received its first emphatic welcome. Many suggestions of Smith's peculiar moral theories are scattered up and down the works of Hume. With regard to Reid, it is only necessary to refer to his own express acknowledgment that it was Hume's sceptical conclusions which first of all startled him into independent inquiry. "I acknowledge," he says, "that I never thought of calling in question the principles commonly received with regard to the human understanding until the *Treatise of Human Nature* was published in the year 1739. The ingenious author of that treatise upon the principles of Locke—who was no sceptic—hath built a system of scepticism which leaves no ground to believe any one thing rather than its contrary. His reasoning appeared to me to be just; there was, therefore, a necessity to call in question the principles on which it was founded, or to admit the conclusion."[1] In Germany, the philosopher Kant, in a well-known passage, makes a similar acknowledgment,[2] so that the two principal philosophical movements of the last century—that of Scotland, which passed likewise into France, and that of Germany, which took its origin in Kant—were due directly to the influence of Hume. If it be argued that these movements represent rather a recoil from Hume's scepticism than any proper development of his ideas, it may be replied that only a thinker of the first

[1] Dedication to his *Inquiry into the Human Mind* (Hamilton's *Reid*, p. 95); see also his letter to Hume below, p. 63.

[2] *Prolegomena*, p. 13.

rank could have called forth such a reaction.[1] But it would be a mistake to look merely to this, and to disregard the intrinsic merit of many of Hume's speculations. The literature of simple antagonism, so plentifully produced in Hume's own day, was little worth, and is now almost forgotten. But more thoughtful writers found in his works, not only doubts, but germs of higher thoughts, and even germs in the doubts themselves. It is doubtful if Kant was acquainted with the *Treatise;*[2] if he had been, he must have found Hume's speculations on Space, Time, Externality, Mathematical Certainty, nearly as fruitful in hints as his discussions on Causation. In our own country it would be difficult to estimate how much of our later philosophy, apart from the line of Reid, is due directly or indirectly to Hume's influence. One important school, at least,—the Associationist,—must be traced to him in direct lineage; but echoes of Hume—vibrations of his thinking—are perceptible in all the empirical philosophies since his day, and never more distinctly than in our own time.

That which gave Hume his special value for subsequent speculation was above all the thoroughness with which he did his work. Hume is commonly and justly described as a sceptic. But the word in his case needs explanation. It will be seen when we come to deal with that topic,[3] that Hume was not a sceptic in the

[1] Mr. Leslie Stephen has said: "The writer who provokes a reaction does as much in generating thought as the writer who propagates his own ideas" (*English Thought in the Eighteenth Century*, ii. p. 5).

[2] Cf. Dr. H. Stirling's *Text-Book to Kant*, p. 16; *contra*, Green's *Introduction to Hume* (Works, i. p. 3).

[3] Chapter V.

sense that he had not a very deep and serious interest in the philosophical questions he discussed, or was not really persuaded that his results, on their negative side at least, and in many positive respects as well, were not established beyond all reasonable cavil. But the peculiarity of Hume's thinking was that, in destroying the beliefs of other people, he could not avoid undermining the authority of reason itself. Reason and natural belief are left by him in irreconcilable opposition; but, more than that, reason gives such an account of its own origin as effectually to destroy its claim to be trusted in any conclusions at which it arrives. But it was precisely through this rigour of his sceptical procedure that Hume was able to do the service he did to philosophy. Starting from principles which, at the time he wrote, were received without question on nearly all hands, he carried these out to their results in such a way as to show that either the principles must be renounced, or the conclusions to which they lead must be accepted. Discarding all rational elements in knowledge, he had to show, in a positive respect, how the ideas which men have—even those which are believed to have a higher origin—can be explained by the simple operation of association and custom; and it may be affirmed with confidence that, if Hume has failed in this task, no other is likely to succeed.

The importance of Hume's philosophy may, therefore, be said to lie in the fact that it is really an *experimentum crucis* as to the possibility of constructing a theory of knowledge which admits no rational or ideal elements, but works solely with empirical factors, like association. Criticism of Hume, on the other hand, resolves itself at every point into the one contention that this endeavour is futile. Hume is a clever writer, but the cleverest writer cannot do impossibilities, and Hume could not write a sentence or paragraph without implicitly overthrowing the system he was advocating. Affecting to ignore the rational nature of man, and seeking to get along without it, he yet is compelled continually to presuppose its existence, and avail himself of its help, in his reasonings and language. Proof of this in regard to Hume is really proof of it in regard to empirical philosophy generally; for theorising which proceeds on empirical lines can do little more than reproduce Hume's arguments, and imitate his methods, while perhaps shutting its eyes to the full bearings and issues of the principles involved, as Hume made them apparent. When even so good a psychologist as Professor William James is found commencing with a "sensation" which, even as we look at it, becomes transformed into an "object," and ere long is part of a "world" of such objects, which by and by are themselves posited as the "causes" of the sensations we began with,—when such a writer can satisfy himself with "cognitive sensations" and the treatment of self as "a stream of mental states," and conclude that "the states of consciousness are all that psychology needs to do her work with," and that "metaphysics or theology may prove the soul to exist, but for psychology the hypothesis of such a substantial principle of unity is superfluous,"[1]—it may be felt how far Hume is from being obsolete, and how imperative is the need of recurrence to his drastic, but at least consistent, logic.

[1] *Text-Book of Psychology*, pp. 202–3, and *passim*.

In view of Professor James's speculations, not to speak of Mr. Spencer's "vivid and faint states" of consciousness, and Mr. Bain's alchemy of association, Hume may be welcomed as a valuable ally in arguing for a more rational theory.

CHAPTER II

LIFE OF HUME—I. TILL THE PUBLICATION OF THE *TREATISE*

THE future philosopher was born on 26th April 1711 (Old Style), "within the Tron Parish"[1] of Edinburgh, where his parents must at the time have been residing. His father, Joseph Hume (or Home), was a border laird of moderate means, but of good family, claiming descent from Lord Home, of Dunglas, who crossed into France with the Douglas in the French wars of the fifteenth century, and lost his life, probably at Verneuil (1423–4). His mother, who, her son says, was "a woman of singular merit,"[2] and for whom he always entertained the warmest affection, was a daughter of Sir David Falconer, President of the Court of Session. The paternal estate was Ninewells, on the northern bank of the Whitadder, in the parish of Chirnside, in Berwickshire. The old, plain mansion, of which a picture is preserved in Chambers's *Book of Days*,[3] was situated on an elevation overlooking the river as it flowed to join the Tweed; and from the declivity in front issued a number of springs, which gave the place its name. Living was plain, and tastes were simple;

[1] Chambers's *Book of Days*, i. p. 555.

[2] Hume's *My Own Life*.

[3] *Ut supra*.

but the Scottish gentry of that time embraced many men of exceptional intelligence and culture,[1] and the library which David found at Ninewells showed that his father must have belonged to that cultured class. Joseph Hume died while David was yet an infant, and he, with an elder brother and sister, were left to the care of their mother, who, though still "young and handsome," devoted herself entirely to their upbringing. As the younger son of the family, his patrimony was necessarily, as he tells us, "very slender."

No details are preserved to us of David's sayings or doings in childhood or youth. The one stray reminiscence that floats down is a reputed saying of his mother's: "Our Davie's a fine, good-natured crater, but uncommon wake-minded." Speculation has naturally been rife as to the meaning of this enigmatical utterance. The riddle is not, perhaps, after all, very difficult to read. The "good-nature" of Hume was proverbial, though his biographer does well to remind us that he "was far from being that docile mass of imperturbability, which so large a portion of the world have taken him for,"[2] and, with regard to the less complimentary part, it may be assumed from what is known of Hume in after life, that he had abstracted ways,[3] and would not readily impress himself on the

[1] Cf. Burton's *Life*, pp. 150 ff. [2] *Ibid.* i. p. 110.

[3] In his quarrel with Rousseau (see below, p. 75) he thus defends himself: "What! because sometimes, when absent in thought, I have a fixed look or stare, you suspect me to be a traitor. . . . Are not most studious men (and many of them more than I) subject to such reveries or fits of silence" (*Works*, i. p. cii). Burton says of him in middle life: "It is pretty clear that he had acquired the outward manner of an absent, good-natured man, unconscious of much that was going on around him" (i. p. 352).

observer in boyhood as of quick and observant parts. His forte was at no time the outward and practical; his reflections, besides, from an early period, were not such as he would be disposed to communicate to others, or as others would easily apprehend. A youthful metaphysician, who, before eighteen, had his doubts of the reality of an external world, and was pondering whether, as Barrie humorously puts it in his *Edinburgh Eleven*, he himself existed "strictly so called," might appear "weak" enough to the average, active-minded people about him. So Hume would keep his thoughts to himself, and content himself with turning on company that good-natured but somewhat vacant expression, which in manhood was noted as a feature of his appearance.[1] As to exterior, we happen to know from his own pen that till the age of twenty he had not the plump, ruddy, healthful look of his maturity, but was a "tall, lean, raw-boned lad."[2]

A silence almost as complete as that which rests on his early days attaches to Hume's school life, and to the period of his university attendance. It is known that he matriculated as an entrant in the class of Greek in Edinburgh University in 1723, at the age of twelve; but no other trace of his curriculum remains. We have it from himself that he "passed through the ordinary course of education with success";[3] and as he elsewhere indicates that "our college education in Scotland, extending little further than the languages, ends commonly when we are about fourteen or fifteen years of age,"[4] it may be presumed that this was the term of his attendance. Thereafter he returned home, and it is

[1] Burton, i. p. 270; see below, p. 42.
[2] *Ibid.* i. p. 34.
[3] *My Own Life.*
[4] Burton, i. p. 31.

during the six or seven years that followed of his residence at Ninewells, diversified by occasional visits to the city,[1] that we begin to see something directly of the workings of his mind, and of the character of his ambitions.

It is still, however, only the growth of a mind we have to study, for then, as throughout life, the merely external interested Hume little. All his biographers have observed how, living in a region of much natural beauty, and rich in romantic associations, he seems to have looked on its scenes without emotion, and hardly allows a trace of its existence, much less of any impulse or impression received from it, to stray into his pages. Nature, indeed, in a way, he did appreciate. In one of his early letters he speaks of the pleasure he found in "an eclogue or georgick of Virgil."[2] But it is nature at second-hand—nature as seen through the eyes, and reflected in the descriptions, of the poets—that interested him, not as stamping fresh impressions on his own soul; nature as a Virgil or a Pope portrayed it, not as a Wordsworth would have *felt* it. Even then he values Virgil less for the images he presents to his imagination, than for the reflections he excites in his mind. There is the same lack of interest in music, painting, and architecture. For none of the plastic arts does he show the slightest original appreciation; and even in awarding the palm of merit in the higher kinds of poetry, his judgments are often ludicrously astray.[3] One quality he does dis-

[1] Burton, i. p. 31. [2] *Ibid.* i. p. 14.

[3] Thus, while Shakespeare incurs the reproach of "barbarism," Home's *Douglas* is thought to redeem the stage from that reproach, and is "the only tragedy," as Wilkie's *Epigoniad* is "the second epic" (next to Milton's), in the language. Burton, i. p. 392; ii. pp. 17, 28. See below, p. 59.

play is the instinct, derived from long and close study of the orators, for polished and flowing composition in prose.

The more remarkable, on account of this indifference to the outward, is the intensity and individuality of the *reflective* life which Hume had already begun to develop. The law had been fixed on as the profession most suitable for one of his industry and sobriety of mind; but his own tastes did not in the least incline him to legal pursuits. "While they fancied," he says, "I was poring upon Voet and Vinnius, Cicero and Virgil were the authors I was secretly devouring."[1] This distaste did not arise from any inherent incapacity for legal studies, but because his ambitions had already (from about his eighteenth year[2]) taken other and very definite directions. "I was early seized," he tells us, in a passage formerly alluded to, "with a passion for literature, which has been the ruling passion of my life, and the great source of my enjoyments";[3] but with this attachment to literature was combined a habit of philosophical reflection, which opened to him visions of conquest and distinction in the region of abstract thought. Three proofs remain to us of the singular development his mind was going through at this period, each fitted to awaken astonishment at the precocity, independence, and maturity of judgment of a youth yet in his teens. The fact that none of the three was intended for the public eye gives them the more value as mirrors of the state of his thoughts.

The first of these evidences is a letter written to a friend, Michael Ramsay, of whom little is known save that he was Hume's life-long correspondent.[4] It is dated

[1] *My Own Life.*
[2] *Letter to Physician*, referred to below.
[3] *My Own Life.*
[4] Burton, i. p. 12.

7th July 1727, when Hume was yet scarcely more than sixteen. It is, however, already composed with deliberation and sententiousness, and pictures the writer as "entirely confined" to himself and to the library at Ninewells for his "diversion." He varies his reading, —"sometimes a philosopher, sometimes a poet,"—and apparently finds his favourites in the Latin authors, as Cicero, Virgil, and Longinus.[1] From the two former he derives the ideal of a life independent of fortune which pretty much remained with him to the end. "The philosopher's wise man and the poet's husbandman," he says, "agree in peace of mind, in a liberty and independency on fortune, and a contempt of riches, power, and glory. Everything is placid and quiet in both; nothing perturbed or disordered." He is well content with his present mode of existence—"I live like a king, pretty much by myself, neither full of action nor perturbation,—*molles somnos*,"—and only fears his happiness may not continue. The panacea against the blows of fortune is to be sought in philosophy—and here we touch the quick of his thought. "This greatness and elevation of soul," he says, "is to be found only in study and contemplation—this alone can teach us to look down on human accidents. You must allow me to talk this, like a philosopher; 'tis a subject I think much on, and could talk all day long of." There is another still more characteristic passage on the nature of his studies which deserves special attention:—

[1] Various indications show that Hume gave assiduous study to the Greek and Latin classics. For his Essay on "The Populousness of Ancient Nations" he claims to have read "almost all the classics, both Greek and Latin" (Burton, i. p. 326).

"Would you have me send in my loose incorrect thoughts? Were such worth the transcribing? All the progress I have made is but drawing the outlines on loose bits of paper: here a hint of a passion; there a phenomenon in the mind accounted for; in another the alteration of these accounts; sometimes a remark upon an author I have been reading; and none of them worth to anybody, and I believe scarcely to myself."

In these "hints" of a passion, and "accountings" for phenomena in the mind, of this singular sixteen-year-old philosopher, it is not too much to say that we have the first germs of the future *Treatise.*

Next to be referred to is an "Historical Essay on Chivalry and Modern Honour," which, if it really belongs, as Mr. Burton thinks, to this youthful period, is a remarkable early anticipation of Hume's later essay style, and a striking evidence of the power he had already attained of looking at historical subjects from an independent point of view. It excellently illustrates his method of seeking an explanation of historical phenomena by tracing them to general principles in human nature; but is not less typical of his habit of finding his means of explanation in principles the least rational and commendable. As at a later stage we find him accounting for the growth of monotheism out of polytheism through the tendency to vulgar flattery;[1] so, in this initial attempt, he finds the key to chivalry—"that monster of romantic chivalry or knight-errantry," as he calls it—in the propensity of the mind, "when smit with any idea of merit or perfection beyond what its faculties can attain," to create an imaginary world, in which it pleases itself with the

[1] See below, p. 199.

fancy of an excellence which does not exist. In the course of the Essay he contrasts Greek with Gothic architecture—the former "plain, simple, and regular, but withal majestic and beautiful"; the latter "a heap of confusion and irregularity"—an evidence of "what kind of monstrous birth this of chivalry must prove."[1]

Of much greater importance, as a clue to Hume's youthful feelings and aims, is the third paper—a sketch of his mental history contained in a letter to a London physician (believed to be Dr. George Cheyne), whom he desired to consult in a crisis of his health. It is doubtful if this mysterious epistle, found neatly written out among his papers, was ever really sent.[2] In belongs in any case to the year 1734. Hume was now twenty-three years of age, but the letter goes back on his whole life, and gives a sort of confidential account of his mental development from the beginning. He first recounts the joy he had felt, after his abandonment of law, at the thought of pushing his fortune in the world as a scholar and philosopher. This lasted till about September 1729, when a sudden chill fell upon his spirits. "All my ardour," he says, "seemed in a moment to be extinguished, and I could no longer raise my mind to that pitch, which formerly gave me such excessive pleasure." His recluse life, and intense application in study, had, it is evident, affected both mind and body; and though, by the use of remedies

[1] Burton, i. p. 22. Mr. Burton observes that "the reflections on Gothic architecture are the commonplaces of the day, uttered by one who was singularly destitute of sympathy with the human intellect, in its early efforts to resolve itself into symmetry and elegance" (p. 26).

[2] See regarding it, Burton, i. pp. 30–9.

and exercise, his strength was gradually restored, so that, as he tells us, from being "tall and lean," he suddenly blossomed out into "the most sturdy, robust, healthful-like fellow you have seen," the inability for sustained and severe mental work remained.[1] This sense of frustrated effort he describes as "such a miserable disappointment I scarce ever remember to have heard of." "Here," he characteristically declares, "lay my greatest calamity. I had no hope of delivering my opinions with such elegance and neatness as to draw on me the attention of the world, and I would rather live and die in obscurity than produce them maimed and imperfect." He asks the advice of the physician, and intimates his intention of entering the employment of a merchant in Bristol—of which more anon.

What further relates to Hume's health may be left aside to look at the remarkable revelations the letter gives of his mental occupations and plans. These are of a nature to dispel any idea of frivolity that might be suggested by his scepticism, and to deepen the impression of sincerity and purpose in his thought and life. Here is how he describes what may be called his mental awakening:—

"I was after that [return from college] left to my own choice in my reading, and found it incline me almost equally to books of reasoning and philosophy, and to poetry and the polite authors. Every one who is acquainted either with the philosophers or critics,

[1] One can hardly help being reminded of the very similar crisis in the life of J. S. Mill, related in his *Autobiography* (p. 134); and of Carlyle's description in his *Sartor* (ii. ch. vii.) and the *Reminiscences* of what he calls his "conversion."

knows that there is nothing yet established in either of these two sciences, and that they contain little more than endless disputes, even in the most fundamental articles. Upon examination of these, I found a certain boldness of temper growing in me, which was not inclined to submit to any authority in these subjects, but led me to seek out some new medium, by which truth might be established. After much study and reflection on this, at last, when I was about eighteen years of age, there seemed to be opened up to me a new scene of thought, which transported me beyond measure, and made me, with an ardour natural to young men, throw up every other pleasure or business to apply entirely to it."

Then ensued the collapse above referred to, in connection with which we have other interesting glimpses of the kind of thoughts that occupied him. The principal passage, however, is the following, which may be said to furnish the programme of his whole life-work in philosophy:—

"Having now time and leisure to cool my inflamed imagination, I began to consider seriously how I should proceed in my philosophical inquiries. I found that the moral philosophy transmitted to us by antiquity laboured under the same inconvenience that has been found in their natural philosophy, of being entirely hypothetical, and depending more on invention than experience; every one consulted his fancy in erecting schemes of virtue and happiness, without regarding human nature, upon which every moral conclusion must depend. This, therefore, I resolved to make my principal study, and the source from which I would derive every truth in criticism as well as in morality.

I believe it is a certain fact, that most of the philosophers who have gone before us, have been overthrown by the greatness of their genius, and that little more is required to make a man succeed in this study, than to throw off all prejudices either for his own opinions or for those of others. At least this is all I have to depend on for the truth of my reasonings, which I have multiplied to such a degree, that within these three years I have scribbled many a quire of paper, in which there is nothing contained but my own inventions. This with the reading most of the celebrated books in Latin, French, and English, and acquiring the Italian, you may think a sufficient business for one in perfect health, and so it would had it been done to any purpose; but my disease was a cruel incumbrance to me."

These paragraphs enable us to appreciate the truth of Mr. Burton's judgment on Hume: "He was an economist of all his talents from early youth: no memoir of a literary man presents a more cautious and vigilant husbandry of the mental powers and acquirements";[1] and to understand a later sentence of the same writer with reference to the *Essays Moral and Political:* "It is into 'The Stoic' that the writer has thrown most of his heart and sympathy; and it is in that sketch that, though probably without intention, some of the features of his own character are pourtrayed."[2]

One outcome of Hume's anxieties on the state of his health was the conviction that his "distemper" was partly due to his sedentary mode of life, and that it would be to his advantage to lay aside his studies for

[1] Burton, i. p. 17. [2] *Ibid.* i. p. 143.

a time, and try the effect of a more active career. The difficulty he felt in carrying out his schemes with his "very slender income" fortified this resolve. He had, as he informs the physician, obtained a recommendation to "a very considerable trader" in Bristol; and he now entered the employment of this gentleman, and continued for some time in his service. It was by no means unusual in that age for younger sons of good families to eke out their scanty means of livelihood in trade; but in Hume's case the experiment was eminently unsuccessful. The merchant, like Hume's mother, not improbably thought his new assistant "uncommon wake-minded" in the duties of his office; and it is not surprising that Hume himself, his head more occupied with the genesis of ideas than with the prices and qualities of goods, after a short trial threw up his situation, and resolved that, come what might, he would confine himself to the line of occupation for which nature had more obviously fitted him. "I went over to France," he says briefly, "with a view of prosecuting my studies in a country retreat; and I then laid that plan of life which I have steadily and successfully pursued. I resolved to make a very rigid frugality supply my deficiency of fortune, to maintain unimpaired my independence, and to regard every object as contemptible except the improvement of my talents in literature."[1]

The sojourn in France to which allusion is here made was a very eventful period in Hume's life. It was during his three years' residence in that country—from 1734 to 1737—that the *Treatise of Human Nature* was composed. After a brief stay in Paris, he

[1] *My Own Life.*

spent some months in the ancient town of Rheims, then took up his abode for two years at La Flèche, where was the Jesuits' College at which, a century and a quarter earlier, the philosopher Descartes had been educated. In these retreats Hume passed his days "very agreeably," but, as one gathers from a letter to his friend Ramsay, filled with acute remarks on the contrast of French and English manners,[1] also very observantly. A feature of some interest in this French sojourn is its bearing on the future Essay on Miracles. When Hume passed through Paris, the city was still stirred on the subject of the alleged miracles at the tomb of the Abbé de Paris, which two years before (1732) had caused great commotion, and had been the subject of prolonged investigation and debate. These miracles, readers of the Essay will remember, furnished Hume with not the least serviceable part of his material for his argument.[2] Then, as he himself relates in a letter to Principal Campbell, it was while at La Flèche, during a walk with a Jesuit in the cloisters of the College, that the idea of the argument itself was suggested to him.

"As my head was full," he says, "of the topics of my *Treatise of Human Nature*, which I was at that time composing, this argument immediately occurred to me, and I thought it very much gravelled my companion; but at last he observed to me that it was impossible for that argument to have any solidity, because it operated equally against the Gospel as against the Catholic miracles;—which observation I thought proper to admit as a sufficient answer."[3]

[1] Burton, i. p. 51.

[2] See below, p. 215.

[3] Preface to Campbell's *Dissertation on Miracles.*

The irony of the last sentence is a trait in Hume's style of which we shall afterwards have abundant examples. It would appear that either then, or soon after, he had reduced his argument to shape, and intended publishing it as part of the *Treatise.* But prudential reasons, as he avows, held him back. He writes on 2nd December 1737 to Henry Home (afterwards Lord Kames): "I enclose some *Reasonings Concerning Miracles* which I once thought of publishing with the rest, but which I am afraid will give too much offence, even as the world is disposed at present." [1]

On his arrival in London, it was Hume's first business to arrange for the publication of his now completed book. It was a daring step for a young man of twenty-six to enter the field of authorship with a work at once so novel and so difficult; but Hume was conscious of the enormous pains he had bestowed on the elaboration of his thoughts; he knew that into this book he had put the best part of *himself*—the whole force and originality of his mind; and he rightly judged that by his success or failure in *this* attempt his reputation as a philosopher must stand or fall. No one will now question that into the *Treatise* Hume has concentrated everything of real value he had to offer in metaphysics and morals; that later works may popularise and polish, but add nothing to the essential content of this earlier effort. It has already been seen how incessantly for years his thoughts had been engrossed with his great project. Now that the time had come for the realisation of his expectations, the tension of his feeling was naturally very great. During the months that negotiations were proceeding with

[1] Burton, i. p. 63.

the booksellers, he was unweariedly engaged in improving the style and diction of his work.[1] He was anxious to have the opinion of others on its merits, and was furnished by Henry Home with an introduction to Bishop Butler, whose *Analogy* had been published the year before; but Butler, to his disappointment, was in the country. "My own [opinion]," he declares, "I dare not trust to; both because it concerns myself, and because it is so variable, that I know not how to fix it. Sometimes it elevates me above the clouds; at other times, it depresses me with doubts and fears; so that, whatever be my success, I cannot be entirely disappointed."[2] One other confession he makes, also having reference to the introduction to Butler, which produces a less favourable impression. "I am," he says, "at present castrating my work, that is, cutting off its nobler parts; that is, endeavouring it shall give as little offence as possible, before which, I could not pretend to put it into the Doctor's hands. This is a piece of cowardice, for which I blame myself, though I believe none of my friends will blame me. But I was resolved not to be an enthusiast in philosophy while I was blaming other enthusiasms."[3] Whether the parts thus excised were restored before publication cannot be affirmed, but, apart from the reasonings on miracles, it may be presumed that they were.

In these preliminaries about a year passed by, and it was not till the 26th of September 1738 that a contract was finally framed between Hume and John Noone, bookseller, of Cheapside, by which the latter bound himself to pay the former £50, with twelve

[1] Burton i. p. 63. [2] *Ibid.* i. p. 65. [3] *Ibid.* i. p. 64.

copies of the book, for the sole right of printing and publishing the first edition, not to exceed 1000 copies. The transaction was, as Mr. Burton says, "on the whole creditable to the discernment and liberality of Mr. Noone."[1] When one reflects that the author was yet young and unknown; that the book was of a kind not adapted to attract the public attention, but more likely to be denounced as a farrago of metaphysical conceits; and that, tested by the value of money in these days, £50 was a considerable sum, the bargain may be called exceedingly generous. This, too, was probably the opinion of the bookseller himself, when, after the publication of the two volumes containing the first and second Books of the *Treatise*, in January 1739, he discovered that, so far from arousing the interest, or exciting the opposition Hume had anticipated, the work had practically no sale whatever. Hume's own succinct account of the matter is: "Never literary attempt was more unfortunate than my *Treatise of Human Nature*. It fell *dead-born* from the press; without reaching such distinction as even to excite a murmur among the zealots."[2] The book was published anonymously; a circumstance which may have helped to doom it to obscurity. The work, in reality, was before its time. The taste capable of appreciating it, and living interest in the questions it discussed, were, in Scotland at least, only beginning to be developed. Half a century later it might have had a different reception. There is no doubt that, meanwhile, Hume was keenly disappointed; though the result did not shake his faith in the merits

[1] Hume, on the other hand, thought he had parted with his book too easily (Letter to Hutcheson, Burton, i. p. 117).

[2] *My Own Life*.

of the book, but only his confidence in the discernment of the public, and in the wisdom of his method of presenting doctrines so abstract and unusual. Within a fortnight of the date of publication he saw that the success of the book was doubtful:—

"I am afraid," he says, "'twill remain so very long. Those who are accustomed to reflect on such abstract subjects are commonly full of prejudices; and those who are unprejudiced are unacquainted with metaphysical reasonings. My principles are also so remote from all the vulgar sentiments on the subjects, that were they to take place, they would produce an almost total revolution in philosophy; and you know, revolutions of this kind are not easily brought about."[1]

While from Ninewells, to which soon after he returned to await developments, he wrote on 1st June to Henry Home:—

"I am not much in the humour of such comparisons at present; having received news from London of the success of my Philosophy, which is but indifferent if I may judge by the sale of the book, and if I may believe my bookseller. I am now out of humour with myself; but doubt not, in a little time, to be only out of humour with the world, like other unsuccessful authors. After all, I am sensible of my folly in entertaining any discontent, much more despair, upon this account, since I could not expect any better from such abstract reasonings; nor, indeed, did I promise myself much better. My fondness for what I imagined my discoveries made me overlook all common rules of prudence; and, having enjoyed the usual satisfaction of

[1] Burton, i. p. 105.

projectors, 'tis but just I should meet with their disappointments."[1]

The *Treatise* did not, indeed, pass altogether unnoticed. A long review of the work, written in a spirit of raillery at Hume's paradoxes, but ending with a handsome acknowledgment of the "incontestable marks of a great capacity," and of "a soaring genius" in the author, appeared in the November issue of a periodical of the day, *The History of the Works of the Learned.* Still, from an observation made long afterwards (1748–9) by his bookseller, Mr. A. Millar, to Hume, that his former publications, "all but the unfortunate *Treatise,*" were beginning to be the subject of conversation,[2] we may gather that Hume did not exaggerate in speaking of his book as falling "deadborn from the press."

The examination of the principles of the work ushered into the world in these discouraging circumstances belongs to later chapters. It is only necessary to indicate here in a few sentences its general character and aim. In its completed form the *Treatise* consists of three Books—the first treating "Of the Understanding," the second, "Of the Passions," and the third, "Of Morals." The volumes published in 1739 comprised the first and second of these Books, and it is in the Book dealing with the Understanding that the really vital part of Hume's system lies. The treatment, as the author acknowledges, is throughout highly abstract; and, what is an even greater disadvantage, is unmethodical and desultory in its exposition of its various topics. But these faults are mainly on the surface. In the thoughts which compose it the work is

[1] Burton, i. p. 108.

[2] *My Own Life.*

powerfully and compactly one; while the style has a vigour and cohesion with the idea, to which a touch of ruggedness only lends additional strength. Its spirit and purpose are best illustrated by quoting from its own pages. Hume opens with a vindication of the right of metaphysical inquiry not easily reconcilable with his later sentiments on the advantages of an "easy and obvious" philosophy:—

"And, indeed," he says, "nothing but the most determined scepticism, along with a great degree of indolence, can justify this aversion to metaphysics. For, if truth be at all within the reach of human capacity, it is certain that it must lie very deep and abstruse; and to hope we shall arrive at it without pains, while the greatest geniuses have failed with the utmost pains, must certainly be esteemed sufficiently vain and presumptuous. I pretend to no such advantage in the philosophy I am going to unfold, and would esteem it a strong presumption against it, were it so very easy and obvious."[1]

His method is announced in the following passage:—

"Here then is the only expedient, from which we can hope for success in our philosophical researches, to leave the lingering tedious method, which we have hitherto followed, and, instead of taking now and then a castle or village on the frontier, to march up directly to the capital or centre of these sciences, to human nature itself; which being once masters of, we may everywhere else hope for an easy victory. . . . In pretending therefore to explain the principles of human nature, we in effect propose a complete system of the sciences, built on a foundation almost entirely new, and the only one

[1] Introduction to *Treatise* (Works, i. p. 6).

on which they can stand with any security. . . . And as the science of man is the only solid foundation for the other sciences, so the only solid foundation we can give to this science itself must be laid on experience and observation."[1]

Human nature, then, we find, is the subject of Hume's investigation, and his method is defined to be the experimental. Already we can perceive the boldness of his enterprise, and the revolutionary character of the conceptions he proposes to expound.

[1] Introduction to *Treatise* (Works, i. p. 8).

CHAPTER III

LIFE OF HUME—II. LITERARY LABOURS TILL THE PUBLICATION OF THE *HISTORY*

HUME was too genuine a philosopher to allow himself to be unduly depressed by the apparent failure of his first attempt at authorship; and, accordingly, he is found without delay setting himself to the preparation for publication of the third Book of his *Treatise*—that on Morals. This part of the work, as following on the treatment of the Understanding and the Passions, deals with moral judgments, and the qualities of virtue and vice in character and actions. It comes, therefore, properly under the general head of an inquiry into human nature, and is conducted on the same principles of rigorous experimental analysis as the previous Books, but without startling the reader with the sceptical paradoxes of the speculative sections. In handling moral questions Hume was entering a field which, since the time of Hobbes, English philosophers had diligently cultivated, and on which, more recently, interest had been concentrated by the lectures of Francis Hutcheson.[1] Not unnaturally, therefore, he was anxious to obtain the opinions and suggestions of the distinguished Glasgow moralist on his perform-

[1] On Hutcheson's popularity, cf. Burton, i. p. 111.

ance, and submitted his manuscript to Dr. Hutcheson for this purpose. An interesting correspondence ensued, chiefly remarkable as showing how tenaciously, while welcoming criticism from others, Hume held by his own ideas. This is characteristic of his epistolary intercourse all through. An incidental result of the correspondence was the opening of an acquaintance between Hume and a "Mr. Smith"—no doubt Adam Smith—then a student at Glasgow, and barely seventeen. Hume, probably at Hutcheson's suggestion, sent Smith a copy of his *Treatise*, a fact which sufficiently indicates the report he had received of the youthful Adam's abilities. It comes out in another letter that Hume was desirous of changing his publisher, and obtained from Hutcheson an introduction to Mr. Longman. It was actually by this publisher that the book was brought out in 1740.

Apart from a stray fact or two, as for instance his attempt to obtain a tutorship in a nobleman's family with a view to travel,[1] Hume's life at this stage is little more than a record of his literary labours. In 1741 appeared in Edinburgh the first volume of his *Essays Moral and Political*, speedily followed by the second volume in 1742.[2] The *Essays*, like the *Treatise*, were published anonymously, but had a distinctly better reception. "The work," Hume says, "was favourably received, and soon made me entirely forget my former disappointment."[3] To Henry Home he writes in 1742: "The *Essays* are all sold in London, as

[1] Burton, i. p. 115.

[2] The publisher of the first two editions was Kincaid, Edinburgh, and of the third, A. Millar, London.

[3] *My Own Life*.

I am informed by two letters from English gentlemen of my acquaintance. There is a demand for them; and, as one of them tells me, Innys, the great bookseller in Paul's Churchyard, wonders there is not a new edition, for that he cannot find copies for his customers. I am also told that Dr. Butler has everywhere recommended them; so that I hope they will have some success."[1] This popularity of the *Essays* is not surprising. They were cast in a mould at that time fashionable. Hume tells us they were originally designed as "weekly papers" on the model of the *Spectator* and the *Craftsman;* but, beyond this, alike in the selection and variety of their subjects, and the finish of their style, they exhibited qualities which, to discerning minds, gave them at once a high rank in literature. As at first published, the volumes contained twenty-seven Essays. Of these as many as eight were gradually dropped, while several new ones were introduced, and other changes made. The third edition, for instance, published in 1748, omitted three of the original Essays, and received an addition of three.[2]

The next years in Hume's history are comparatively uneventful. Two occurrences slightly break the monotony. In 1743–4 some stir was caused by a sermon published by the Rev. Dr. Leechman, of Beith, on Prayer, followed by the appointment of its author to the Chair of Divinity in the University of Glasgow. The sermon, which resolved the efficacy of prayer into its reflex influence on the mind of the worshipper, was submitted to Hume for suggestions through his friend, William (afterwards Baron) Mure, of Caldwell, and the

[1] Burton, i. p. 143.

[2] On the history of the Editions, see Appendix.

reply is interesting, as showing how far Hume's mind was severed from everything in religion, except, as he says, "the practice of morality, and the assent of the understanding to the proposition *that God exists*."[1] Affection to Deity cannot, he thinks, owing to the invisibility and incomprehensibility of its object, be required of man as his duty, and, even "were devotion never so much admitted, prayer must still be excluded." He shows that Dr. Leechman's doctrine reduces prayer to "a kind of rhetorical figure," and by encouraging the idea that prayers have a direct influence, "leads directly, and even unavoidably, to blasphemy."[2] On the main point, therefore, though from opposite sides, Hume and Dr. Leechman's theological opponents were at one. The other event which gives a little colour to this period is the effort made by Hume to secure the appointment to the chair of "Ethics and Pneumatic Philosophy" in the University of Edinburgh. The occupant of the chair, Dr. (afterwards Sir John) Pringle, had been appointed physician to the Earl of Stair, Commander of the British Forces in the Low Countries, and, in accordance with a loose practice of these times, had been for two years absent from his duties in the University. The Town Council of Edin-

[1] Burton, i. p. 162. The description given by the admiring biographer (Rev. James Wodrow) of Dr. Leechman of his method as Professor is very characteristic: "No dictatorial opinion, no infallible or decisive judgment on any great controverted point was ever delivered from that theological chair. After the point had undergone a full discussion, none of the students yet knew the opinion of this venerable professor, in any other way than by the superior weight of the arguments he had brought under their view; so delicately scrupulous was he to throw any bias at all upon ingenuous minds, in their inquiries after sacred truth" (Preface to *Sermons*).

[2] *Ibid.* i. pp. 163–4.

burgh, to which he offered his resignation, thought it necessary that at least a term be put to his further absence, and in March 1745 he actually did resign. When the vacancy was in prospect, Hume was induced to put himself forward as a candidate (August 1744), and, backed by the Provost's influence, thought himself secure of the appointment. "I found presently," he writes, "that I should have the whole Council on my side, and that, indeed, I should have no antagonist."[1] Opposition, however, soon showed itself, and from unexpected quarters. "The accusation of heresy, deism, scepticism, atheism, etc. etc. etc.," he says, "was started against me; but never took, being bore down by the contrary opinion of all the good company in town."[2] Much more to his surprise, he found that "Mr. Hutcheson and even Mr. Leechman" were in the ranks of those who agreed that he "was a very unfit person for such an office."[3] The efforts also of the "good company" to persuade the public that Hume was no heretic, deist, or sceptic, must have failed;[4] for, when the vacancy actually occurred, his name was not even mentioned. The post was given in June 1745 to William Cleghorn, who had taught in Dr. Pringle's absence.

A disagreeable episode in Hume's career fills up the interval from April 1745 to April 1746. The Marquis of Annandale,—last of that title,—a man of excitable disposition, and, as it proved, in the first stages of

[1] Burton, i. p. 166. [2] *Ibid.* i. p. 167. [3] *Ibid.*

[4] *Ibid.* p. 178: "I am informed that such a popular clamour has been raised against me in Edinburgh, on account of scepticism, heterodoxy, and other hard names, which confound the ignorant, that my friends find some difficulty in working out the point of my professorship, which once appeared so easy."

insanity, had been attracted by Hume's *Essays*, and, early in 1745, invited Hume to become his companion at his residence at Weldhall, near St. Albans, in Hertfordshire. He sent Hume £100, and finally an arrangement was come to, by which Hume was to receive £300 a year so long as the connection lasted. The position, though not an enviable one, had its obvious advantages, and Hume might have endured it, but for the offensive tyranny of a Captain Vincent, a relation of the Dowager-Marchioness, to whom was entrusted the management of the Marquis's affairs. The self-seeking designs of this man Hume early detected and sought to counteract, with the result that Vincent, who at first had been friendly, became his bitter enemy, plotted to reduce his salary by one-half, and made his situation as servile and galling as a man of coarse nature, invested with authority, could. The perturbation of spirit occasioned by his affronts leads Hume to break out in his correspondence into quite unusual strains. He had resisted his suspicions of Vincent, he tells us, as he would "a temptation of the devil," and in his excitement he thus accosts Sir James Johnstone: "God forgive you, dear Sir, God forgive you, for neither coming to us, nor writing to us."[1] The Marquis's temper became daily more uncontrollable, and when self-respect could stand the indignities heaped upon him no longer, Hume took his departure. A sequel to the quarrel was a claim put in by Hume for £75 of arrears of salary, the somewhat sordid dispute in regard to which dragged on till at least 1761. It is not known how it was settled.

Hume's next experiences were of a much more

[1] Burton, i. p. 183.

pleasant order. They relate to his connection with General St. Clair in the capacity of secretary, first, during a naval expedition conducted in 1746 against the coasts of France; and, second, during a military embassy in 1748 to the Court of Turin, the progress of which gave him an opportunity of seeing a large part of the Continent. These two years Hume speaks of as "almost the only interruptions which my studies have received during the course of my life"[1]—language which it is difficult to reconcile with his later occupations in France and England. The expedition first named had a somewhat inglorious history. It was originally intended to be sent against the French possessions in Canada; then resolved itself into a descent on the coast of France itself. It set sail on 14th September 1746, and landed its forces on the 20th at the town of Fort L'Orient, on the coast of Brittany. The attempt to compel the town to surrender proved a failure. Sickness set in, and in less than a week it was found necessary to raise the siege, and retreat to the fleet. The expedition soon after returned home. In addition to his position as secretary, Hume was appointed by the General Judge-advocate to all the forces under his command He formed, besides, valuable acquaintances, and saw a little of actual warfare. The most interesting point in his correspondence in this period is the indication of certain "historical projects,"[2] which we can trace rapidly settling into the purpose of writing a History.

The year 1747 was spent at Ninewells, an interval of which his biographer takes advantage to introduce some specimens of Hume's versification, and to discuss

[1] *My Own Life.*

[2] Burton, i. p. 221.

the probability of his ever having been in love. Assuredly, if the Clarindas and Lauras of Hume's muse were real persons, his passion for them must have been of a very mild sort; nor, while avowing himself fond of the society of "modest women," does he ever seem to have been peculiarly susceptible to female charms. In his *Essays*, as Mr. Burton says, "he frequently discusses the passion of love, dividing it into its elements about as systematically as if he had subjected it to a chemical analysis, and laying down rules regarding it as distinctly and specifically as if it were a system of logic."[1]

It was in the year following, 1748, that General St. Clair showed his appreciation of Hume's previous services by inviting him to attend him as his secretary on his mission to Turin. This was an opportunity not to be lost, though it was not without regret that Hume laid aside the plans of study he had formed. We now hear from him distinctly, "I have long had an intention, in my riper years, of composing some history";[2] but he was wise enough to see that some wider experiences of cities and men, and of "the intrigues of the Cabinet," would be a valuable aid in the carrying out of his design. Nor did the experience of the next few months disappoint his expectations. His letters begin to show an unwonted interest in people and things, and his descriptions of the cities through which he passed —of the Hague, Breda, Nimeguen, Cologne, Bonn, Coblentz, Frankfort, Ratisbon, on to Vienna, Trent, Mantua, and finally Turin—are lively and entertaining. His enthusiasm for Virgil comes out at Mantua: "We are now on classic ground; and I have kissed the

[1] Burton, i. p. 231. [2] *Ibid.* i. p. 236.

earth that produced Virgil, and have admired those fertile plains that he has so finely celebrated."[1] But it is noted that he never once condescends to mention any of the fine specimens of Gothic architecture he met with in his progress—not even the imposing fragment of the Cathedral of Cologne. Hume's appearance on this embassy, clad in military scarlet, seems to have afforded some entertainment to his friends, if one may judge from the grotesque description given of him by that versatile Irish politician, Lord Charlemont:—

"Nature, I believe," says this witness, "never formed any man more unlike his real character than David Hume. The powers of physiognomy were baffled by his countenance; neither could the most skilful in that science pretend to discover the smallest trace of the faculties of his mind in the unmeaning features of his visage. His face was broad and fat, his mouth wide, and without any other expression than that of imbecility. His eyes vacant and spiritless, and the corpulence of his whole person, was far better fitted to communicate the idea of a turtle-eating alderman, than of a refined philosopher. His speech in English was rendered ridiculous by the broadest Scotch accent, and his French was, if possible, still more laughable; so that Wisdom most certainly never disguised herself before in so uncouth a garb. Though now near fifty years of age [he was thirty-seven], he was healthy and strong, but his health and strength, far from being advantageous to his figure, instead of manly comeliness, had only the appearance of rusticity. His wearing a uniform added greatly to his natural awkwardness, for he wore it like a grocer of the train bands."[2]

[1] Burton, i. p. 265.

[2] *Ibid.* i. p. 270.

The mission to Turin was superseded by the treaty of Aix-la-Chapelle on 7th October, and at some uncertain date thereafter Hume returned to London. There, soon after his arrival, he received a great blow in the news of the death of his mother. The reality of his emotion, and the spirit in which he met the bereavement, are attested by the following narrative, by Dr. Carlyle, of Inveresk, which also sufficiently disposes of certain absurd stories set afloat by unscrupulous inventors:—

"David and he [the Hon. Mr. Boyle, brother of the Earl of Glasgow] were both in London at the period when David's mother died. Mr. Boyle, hearing of it, soon after went into his apartment, for they lodged in the same house, where he found him in the deepest affliction, and in a flood of tears. After the usual topics of condolence, Mr. Boyle said to him, 'My friend, you owe this uncommon grief to having thrown off the principles of religion; for if you had not, you would have been consoled with the firm belief that the good lady, who was not only the best of mothers, but the most pious of Christians, was completely happy in the realms of the just.' To which David replied, 'Though I throw out my speculations to entertain the learned and metaphysical world, yet in other things I do not think so differently from the rest of the world as you imagine.'"[1]

Notwithstanding this utterance, there is no reason to suppose that Hume's general attitude of disbelief in the Christian religion was anything but entirely serious, or ever altered. Of this, as well as of the unchanged character of his philosophical foundations, a conclusive

[1] Burton, i. pp. 293–4.

proof had just been given by the publication in 1748, while he was on his way to Turin, of the recast and popularised version of his speculations under the title of *Philosophical Essays concerning Human Understanding*, subsequently modified to *Enquiry concerning the Human Understanding*. The book was published in London by Andrew Millar. At first it bore simply to be by 'the Author of the *Essays Moral and Political*.' But in November of the same year a new edition was issued with the author's name. At first the *Enquiry* seemed fated to attract as little attention as the *Treatise;* but Hume's growing reputation, and the bolder pronouncements of the book on subjects affecting revealed religion, soon led to wider notice, and hostile criticism. Hume's own design was that this simplified and improved form of his system should take the place of his older work, which he now desired to withdraw from circulation. His feeling on this point is best expressed in the "Advertisement" prefixed to the book in the posthumous and authoritative edition of 1777. He there rebukes the adversaries for directing "all their batteries against that juvenile work, whieh the author never acknowledged, and have affected to triumph in any advantages which, they imagined, they had obtained over it"—"a practice," he says, "very contrary to all rules of candour and fair dealing, and a strong instance of those polemical artifices which a bigoted zeal thinks itself authorised to employ." Now, however, he expressly desires "that the following Pieces may alone be regarded as containing his philosophical sentiments and principles."

It has already been seen that Hume's wishes with regard to the neglect of his *Treatise* have not been fulfilled. It is not "bigoted zeal," but that world of philosophy and letters to which he appealed, which has refused to let the older work drop out of sight, or be displaced by the newer *Enquiry*. It is not simply that the *Treatise* is by far the abler and more vigorous and original work; beyond this there is the fact that the second work really alters nothing in the philosophical basis of the first, while it leaves out much that is necessary for the understanding of the system as a whole. It was not, after all, the subject-matter, but the lack of popularity, of his earlier work which distressed Hume; he claims only that, in the newer handling, "some negligences in his former reasoning, and more in the expression, are, he hopes, corrected." Had it been given to him to foresee the estimate that posterity would put upon his *Treatise*, in comparison with its later echo, the suppression of it is the last thing he would have desired. The utmost that can be claimed is, that where differences of view emerge, the later statement shall be taken as the final one. One advantage, at least, of the *Enquiry* is, that it helps to throw into relief the things that Hume himself thought of most importance in his philosophy. While much that is in the *Treatise* is omitted, we have, sometimes in briefer, occasionally in more expanded form, a re-statement of his theories on the origin of ideas, on association, on causation, on the idea of necessary connection, on liberty and necessity, etc.; while important additions are made in the Essays on "Miracles" and on "a Particular Providence and a Future State."[1] Two extracts will suffice at this

[1] Mr. Burton mistakenly says: "It was in the *Inquiry concerning the Human Understanding* that Hume promulgated the theory of

stage to show the general spirit of the work—one from the commencement, the other from the close.

The first suggests comparison with Kant:—

"The only method of freeing learning at once from these abstruse questions is to inquire seriously into the nature of human understanding, and show, from an exact analysis of its powers and capacity, that it is by no means fitted for such remote and abstruse subjects. We must submit to this fatigue, in order to live at ease ever after; and must cultivate true metaphysics with some care, in order to destroy the false and adulterated."[1]

The second is the drastic conclusion, dear to Professor Huxley:—

"If we take in our hand any volume, of school divinity, or metaphysics, for instance; let us ask, *Does it contain any abstract reasoning concerning quantity or number?* No. *Does it contain any experimental reasoning concerning matter of fact and existence?* No. Commit it then to the flames; for it can contain nothing but sophistry and illusion."[2]

During 1749 and 1750 Hume lived peacefully at Ninewells, though brain and pen were still unceasingly busy. His correspondence in these years with Dr. Clephane, of London, Colonel Abercromby, and others, reveals a vein of sportiveness not ordinarily found in his compositions.[3] We find him more seriously engaged

Association which called forth so much admiration of its simplicity, beauty, and truth" (i. p. 286). The doctrine of Association is even more fully developed in the earlier *Treatise*.

[1] Works, iv. p. 9. [2] *Ibid.* p. 187.

[3] Cf. his squib on Fraser in connection with the Westminster Election, and his "Bellman's Petition" (Burton, i. pp. 307–18).

in earnest preparation of his *Political Discourses*,[1] published two years later; and his letters to Sir Gilbert Elliot, a gentleman of great accomplishment, reveal also that by this time (1751) he had composed his *Dialogues concerning Natural Religion*,[2] of which a good deal will afterwards be heard. In these *Dialogues*, which were not published till after his death, the cause of Theism is upheld by Cleanthes, and Hume tells his correspondent that whatever he can think of to strengthen that side of the argument will be most acceptable to him.[3] Sir Gilbert gave him his views at length,[4] but few will regard the *Dialogues* as a prop to theistic belief. The chief outcome of this period of labour, however, was the publication in 1751 of his *Enquiry concerning the Principles of Morals*, which answers to the third Book of the original *Treatise*, and completes, with the exception of the Dissertation on the Passions,[5] the recasting of that earlier work. The publisher was again Mr. Millar. In Hume's own judgment, this was, of all his works, "historical, philosophical, and literary, incomparably the best."[6] Posterity may not endorse this opinion, but most will allow that, from a purely literary point of view, the work is elaborated and polished to a high degree. Hume had now clearly grasped the principle of "utility" as a key to the phenomena of morals, and developed his thesis

[1] Burton, i. pp. 301–4. A correspondence with Montesquieu belongs also to this period.

[2] See below, pp. 200 ff.

[3] Burton, pp. 308–36.

[4] His letter is given in Note CCC. to Dugald Stewart's *Dissertation*.

[5] See below, pp. 58, 169.

[6] *My Own Life*. Hume gives the date of publication as 1752. This may be due to the difference in the English and Scotch ways of reckoning. 1752 was the year of the change of the Calendar.

with a skill which made his book a landmark in the history of discussion on the subject. As before, the work attracted little attention at the time, though a reply from the pen of James (afterwards Professor) Balfour, of Pilrig, appeared in 1753, the ability and courtesy of which induced Hume to seek the acquaintance of the author.

It was probably before the appearance of the last-named work that Hume effected the change of his residence to Edinburgh, which opens a new period in his career. The immediate occasion of this step was his brother's marriage;[1] but the removal was prompted also by a natural desire to be in a city already rising to distinction as an abode of letters, and affording exceptional facilities for the carrying out of his literary designs. Hume was now, moreover, in comparatively easy circumstances. He was, he tells us, the happy possessor of about £1000.[2] He writes to his friend Ramsay (June 1751) that he could reckon on an income of about £50 a year, and by joining with his sister, who brought another £30, was able, with frugality, to set up a house in the capital.[3] Accordingly, somewhat later in the year, he removed, as he informs us, "from the country to the town, the true scene for a man of letters."[4] His first settled residence (of which, however, he does not seem to have taken possession till about May 1752)[5] was in "Riddell's Land," near the head of the West Bow, in the Lawn-

[1] Burton, ii. p. 50.

[2] *My Own Life.*

[3] Burton, i. p. 342.

[4] *My Own Life.*

[5] In a letter of date 5th January 1753, from this address, he speaks of himself as having set up house about "seven months ago" (Burton, i. p. 377).

market. Next year he removed to "Jack's Land," another of Edinburgh's tall tenements,[1] in the Canongate. Here he remained till his purchase, in 1762, of a house of his own in James's Court.

It was shortly after this removal to Edinburgh, in 1752, that Hume published his *Political Discourses,* mostly on subjects of Political Economy, and as remarkable in their grasp of sound principles, as in their anticipations of some of the later doctrines of Adam Smith in his *Wealth of Nations.* He speaks of this book as "the only work of mine that was successful on its first publication," and informs us that "it was well received abroad and at home."[2] An indication of this acceptance is that a translation of it was soon made into French. The book was published by Kincaid, of Edinburgh, and in its original form consisted of twelve Essays.[3] One of these on "The Populousness of Ancient Nations" affords striking evidence of the author's wide range of reading, and faculty of just observation, and evoked a good deal of controversy. The Essay on an "Ideal Commonwealth" which closes the volume, on the other hand, as conspicuously illustrates Hume's limitations as a constructive thinker. It is as curious a day-dream as ever emanated from the brain of a really sensible man.

Meanwhile, the winter of 1751 had seen Hume involved in a fresh attempt to obtain the dignity of Professor. The Chair of Logic had become vacant by

[1] "The term 'Land,'" says Mr. Burton, "applied to one of those edifices—some of them ten or twelve stories high—in which the citizens of Edinburgh, pressed upwards as it were by the increase of the population within a narrow circuit of walls, made staircases supply the place of streets, and erected perpendicular thoroughfares" (i. p. 343).

[2] *My Own Life.*

[3] On the Editions, see Appendix.

the transference of Adam Smith to the Chair of Moral Philosophy, and Hume's friends, with his concurrence, interested themselves to secure the position for him, but, as before, in vain. The disappointment which this occasioned was partially soothed next year (1752) by his election to the office of librarian to the Faculty of Advocates in Edinburgh, at a salary of £40 a year. For this post also a contest was waged, which, if Hume is not exaggerating, was attended with a good deal of excitement. "'Twas vulgarly given out," he writes to Dr. Clephane, "that the contest was between Deists and Christians, and when the news of my success came to the Playhouse, the whisper ran round that the Christians were defeated. Are you not surprised that we could keep our popularity, notwithstanding this imputation, which our friends could not deny to be well founded?"[1] The appointment was one of great value to Hume, as aiding his historical researches; but he did not long retain it. Resentment at a slight passed upon him by the curators, led him, two years later, voluntarily to transfer the emoluments of the office to the blind poet Blacklock;[2] and in January 1757 he resigned it altogether.[3]

The ten years succeeding the publication of the *Political Discourses* had really but one absorbing occupation—the composition and publication of the successive volumes of the work which at length raised Hume to the height of a truly European fame, if it also exposed him to the blasts of adverse criticism at home. This was his *History of England*, extending, when complete, from the invasion of Julius Cæsar to the Revolution of 1688. Hume had begun by giving

[1] Burton, i. p. 371. [2] *Ibid.* i. p. 371. [3] *Ibid.* i. p. 393.

to the world his metaphysical and moral speculations. He had next developed in his *Essays* his theories on taste, on politics, on economics; and had practically completed his message on all these heads. He was now to enter a field for success in which new powers were needed, and in which his principles would be at once applied and tested. Hume had but a poor opinion of the performances of his predecessors in the domain of English history. "You know," he writes to Dr. Clephane, "that there is no post of honour in the English language more vacant than that of history. Style, judgment, impartiality, care—everything is wanting to our historians; and even Rapin, during this latter period, is extremely deficient."[1] On the other hand, he entertained no doubt at all of his own ability to produce a history worthy of the subject and of literature; and, despite the glaring defects of the work, to which reference will afterwards be made, posterity has on the whole accorded him the niche in the temple of fame he coveted. A remarkable circumstance was the extraordinary rapidity with which the successive instalments of the *History* were composed. Hume conceived it wiser, though he afterwards regretted his decision,[2] to begin with the period of the Stuarts, and before the end of 1754 he had published the first volume of his *History of Great Britain*, a quarto of 473 pages, containing the reigns of James I. and Charles I. Notwithstanding the discouragement which, we shall see, the reception of this first volume caused him, he had produced by 1756 his second volume, bringing down the narrative to the Revolution of 1688. His first volume was published by Hamilton,

[1] Burton, ii. p. 378. [2] *Ibid.* ii. p. 38.

Balfour, & Neill, Edinburgh; his second, by Andrew Millar, London, who thereafter secured the copyright of both, and became the publisher of the subsequent volumes.[1] Having finished his history of the Stuarts, he reverted to the period of the Tudors, and in 1759 published the two volumes of his history of the House of Tudor. This was followed at no greater interval than 1762 by two other quartos, comprising the history of England from Julius Cæsar till the accession of Henry VII. Quartos, in fact, in this period of phenomenal activity, literally *flowed* from Hume. There remained, according to the original plan, the period succeeding the Revolution, and for a considerable time Hume had the preparation of this concluding part of his work before his thoughts. Bookseller and friends urged him to the task;[2] but his visit to France and other engagements intervened, and all the pressure they could exert failed to bring him to set about the undertaking in right earnest. The project was finally abandoned; and, apart from corrections and alterations of his volumes, Hume's literary productivity may be said to have ceased in 1762.

The merits and defects of the *History* will be considered in their proper place;[3] but a few words may be said here on the reception accorded to the work

[1] It would appear that Hume was to receive from Hamilton £1200 for the *three* volumes originally projected, and probably got £400 for the first. Thereafter his transactions are with Millar, who appears to have given him (Burton, ii. p. 37) £700 for the second volume; also for copyright of the two volumes the sum of 800 guineas, or £840. His total remuneration for the Stuart volumes was therefore £1940. His Tudors were offered for £700, but this when only *one* volume was in view. Cf. Hill's *Letters to Strahan*, pp. 13–15.

[2] Burton, ii. pp. 135, 147, 244, 392, etc.

[3] Chapter XI.

produced under these remarkable conditions. Hume's own account of the reception of the original volume is as follows:—

"I was, I own, sanguine in my expectations of the success of this work. I thought I was the only historian that had at once neglected present power, interest, and authority, and the cry of popular prejudices; and as the subject was suited to every capacity, I expected proportional applause. But miserable was my disappointment. I was assailed by one cry of reproach, disapprobation, and even detestation: English, Scotch, and Irish, Whig and Tory, Churchman and Sectary, Free-thinker and Religionist, Patriot and Courtier, united in their rage against the man who had presumed to shed a generous tear for the fate of Charles I. and the Earl of Strafford; and after the first ebullitions of their fury were over, what was still more mortifying, the book seemed to sink into oblivion. Mr. Millar told me that in a twelvemonth he sold only forty-five copies of it."[1]

Hume goes on to confess that this unexpected reception of his book "discouraged" him; so much so, that, had it not been that war was at the time breaking out between France and England, he would certainly have retired to some provincial town of the former kingdom, have changed his name, and never more have returned to his native country.[2] Here, however, as in other instances, his excessive desire for popularity leads him to exaggerate the ill-success of his volume.[3] Hostility,

[1] *My Own Life.*

[2] *Ibid.*

[3] Burton observes: "The literary success that would satisfy Hume required to be of no small amount. Though neither, in any sense, a vain man, nor a caterer for ephemeral applause, he was greedy of praise,

intense and widespread, the *History*, indeed, did encounter; but the opposition rather gave it notoriety than doomed it to oblivion. Hume's own letters show that, in Scotland at least, it had a remarkably cordial reception. "The sale," he writes to Adam Smith in December 1754, "has been very great in Edinburgh; but how it goes on in London, we have not been precisely informed."[1] And to the Earl of Balcarras on same date (17th December), "I am very proud that my *History*, even upon second thoughts, appears to have something tolerable in your lordship's eyes. It has been very much canvassed and read here in town, as I am told; and it has full as many inveterate enemies as partial defenders. The misfortune of a book, says Boileau, is not the being ill-spoken of, but the not being spoken of at all. The sale has been very considerable here, about four hundred and fifty copies in five weeks. How it has succeeded in London I cannot precisely tell; only I observe that some of the weekly papers have been busy with me."[2] In truth, as we shall see, Hume had no reason to be surprised at the amount or violence of the opposition his *History* called forth. It had, as every critic admits, many of the qualities of a first-class historical work. But its excellences were counterbalanced by equally serious defects. Hume prides himself on nothing so much as on his "impartiality"; yet "impartiality," in the real sense of the word, is precisely the quality in which the work is conspicuously wanting. For the higher range of motives he has, as we shall see, little comprehension;

and what would have been to others pre-eminent success, appears to have, in his eyes, scarcely risen above failure" (i. p. 403; cf. ii. p. 262).

[1] Burton, i. p. 411. [2] *Ibid.* i. p. 412.

hence, while his "generous tear" drops for Strafford and Charles, he has no insight into the genius and meaning of a great religious movement like Puritanism, or into a character like that of Cromwell, who is to him throughout what he names him on his first appearance—"this fanatical hypocrite."[1] Yet Hume was genuinely amazed that any one should impugn the justice, or challenge the perfect impartiality, of his judgments!

The second volume of the *History*—that dealing with the Commonwealth, Charles II., and James II.—"happened," Hume says, "to give less displeasure to the Whigs, and was better received. It not only rose itself, but helped to buoy up its unfortunate brother."[2] It was really written with more caution. Hume was resolved, as he assured his publisher, to "give no further umbrage to the godly."[3] The publication of the volumes of the Tudors, on the other hand, revived all the former animosities. "The clamour against this performance," he says, "was almost equal to that against the history of the two first Stuarts."[4] The reign of Elizabeth was particularly obnoxious. The fame of Hume, however, was by this time too securely established to be shaken by these outbursts of disapprobation. Still the critics had not misjudged. Every new issue of the volumes showed that the spirit pervading them was one wholly antipathetic to genuine love of liberty. It is noticed that nearly all the changes in later editions are on the side adverse to popular rights. Hume himself says: "In above a hundred alterations which further study, reading, and reflection, engaged

[1] *History*, ch. li. (vol. vi. p. 274).
[2] *My Own Life*.
[3] Burton, i. p. 416.
[4] *Ibid.* i. p. 416.

me to make in the reigns of the first two Stuarts, I have made all of them invariably to the Tory side."[1] Nothing need be said of the volumes of the *History* prior to the period of the Tudors. These are the least original and valuable of the whole, and need to be corrected at every point from later research.

[1] *My Own Life;* cf. Burton, ii. pp. 73-8, 144-7, 434.

CHAPTER IV

LIFE OF HUME—III. FROM THE PUBLICATION OF THE *HISTORY* TILL HIS DEATH.

A FEW events, partly personal and partly literary, which belong to the period when Hume was occupied with his *History*, have still to be mentioned. Hume's sceptical opinions were well known, and in 1755–6, attempts were made, at the instance of a polemical individual, the Rev. George Anderson, to bring him, in conjunction with Lord Kames,[1] under the censure of the General Assembly of the Church. The Assembly went so far as to pass a resolution expressive of the Church's "utmost abhorrence" of "impious and infidel principles," and of "the deepest concern on account of the prevalence of infidelity and immorality, the principles of which have been, to the disgrace of our age and nation, so openly avowed in several books published of late in this country, and which are but too well known among us."[2] When, however, in the following year, the attack was renewed in a Committee of Assembly against Hume personally, the proposal to send up an overture on the subject was rejected.[3]

[1] Kames's *Essays* had really been written in opposition to Hume.

[2] Burton, i. p. 429.

[3] The indefatigable Anderson tried afterwards to have the publishers

The next year (1757) saw the publication by Mr. Millar of a volume consisting of *Four Dissertations*, which, as it turned out afterwards, had a curious and complicated history. The Dissertations in question were on "The Natural History of Religion," "The Passions" (taking the place of the corresponding Book in the *Treatise*), "Tragedy," and "The Standard of Taste." Originally, it would seem, the volume was meant to include a Dissertation on "Geometry," probably with reference to the discussions on that subject in the older work. Then (excluding Geometry), it was intended to embrace, along with the first three of the above-named Essays, two others on "Suicide" and "The Immortality of the Soul." These Essays were actually printed as part of the volume, but were subsequently suppressed, and in their room was inserted, finally, the disquisition on "The Standard of Taste." The fact of the suppression was brought to light by the unauthorised publication, in 1783, of the two Essays, with adverse comments, by a person who had surreptitiously obtained copies of them.[1] The motive of the suppression is sufficiently obvious from their character: one a thoroughgoing defence of the lawfulness of suicide; the other a sceptical undermining of the arguments for a future life. The Essay on Immortality is not rendered less distasteful by its ironical allusions at the beginning and the end to the obligations of mankind to divine revelation.[2]

The volume of *Dissertations* casts light on Hume's mind in other ways. As originally printed, it was

of Lord Kames's *Essays* arraigned before the Presbytery, but died before the case came on.

[1] Cf. Burton, ii. p. 202. See Appendix. [2] See below, p. 207.

introduced by an affectionate dedication to John Home, who was at the time in trouble with the Church over the production of his tragedy of *Douglas* on the stage in Edinburgh; and Hume was persuaded to suppress this dedication, lest it should further compromise his friend's prospects. Almost immediately he repented his decision, moved probably by the knowledge that Home intended resigning his charge at Athelstaneford. But the edition was issued, and it was only later that the Dedication could be restored. Its inflated language is a characteristic illustration of Hume's curious blindness in matters of literary judgment, where personal friendship, and especially anything Scottish, was concerned. He thus addresses Home: "You possess the true Theatric Genius of Shakespeare and Otway, refined from the unhappy Barbarism of the one, and the Licentiousness of the other."[1] He writes to Adam Smith concerning the tragedy itself: "When it shall be printed (which will be soon), I am persuaded it will be esteemed the best, and by French critics the only tragedy in the language"![2] An instance of the like overweening estimate of the performances of his friends occurs about the same time in his extravagant appreciation of the *Epigoniad* of the poet Wilkie. To Hume's mind Wilkie was almost the equal of Homer. His production was "the second epic poem in our language." "It is certainly," he says, "a most singular production, full of sublimity and genius, adorned by a noble, harmonious, forcible, and even correct versification."[3] This generous temper had no doubt its praise-

[1] Cf. Hill's *Letters to Strahan*, p. 16. [2] Burton, ii. p. 17.

[3] *Ibid.* ii. pp. 25–28. Burton says: "No Scotchman could write a

worthy side, enabling Hume to take a disinterested delight in the literary successes even of those who stood to him more nearly in the position of rivals. He rejoiced unfeignedly in the chorus of approval which greeted the appearance of his friend Dr. Robertson's *History of Scotland* (1758), and in the welcome accorded to *The Theory of Moral Sentiments* of Adam Smith (1759).[1] He even seems for a time (though not quite unreservedly) to have yielded to belief in the genuineness of the poems of "Ossian," in defence of which Dr. Hugh Blair had written a learned Dissertation. Reflection soon led him to a very different judgment on this last point. There is preserved from his pen an "Essay on the Authenticity of Ossian's Poems," in which the claims of the poems to antiquity are mercilessly demolished. The Essay was not published in his lifetime; but it is characteristic that he continues to write to Blair as if his mind was still in the balance on the question.[2] From the end of 1758 till about November 1759, Hume resided in London, superintending the publication of his volumes on the Tudors, and rendering service to Dr. Robertson in seeing his *History of Scotland* through the press. He had even at one time (1757) the thought of taking up his permanent residence in London.[3] Edinburgh, how-

book of respectable talent without calling forth his loud and warm eulogiums. Wilkie was to be the Homer, Blacklock the Pindar, and Home the Shakespeare, or something still greater, of his country" (p. 31).

[1] Burton, ii. pp. 32, 43, 49, 55, etc.

[2] Hume's correspondence with Blair, and the Essay referred to, are given in the Appendix to vol. i. of Burton's *Life*. But see also vol. ii. pp. 175, 180, 196, 267, 288; and his letter to Gibbon, p. 485.

[3] Burton, ii. p. 39.

ever, was still the place most congenial to him. In 1762, as formerly mentioned, he changed his residence in that city to a house he had acquired in James's Court, a large square enclosure, into which one still enters by a "close" from the Lawnmarket. Tall buildings surrounded the Court. The house which Hume occupied was on the third storey on the northern side, and from its windows commanded a fine view of the lake in the hollow below, and of the open spaces beyond, now covered by the New Town of Edinburgh. The erection of which his domicile formed part has since been replaced by the "Offices" of what, formerly the Free Church, is now the United Free Church of Scotland. Here Hume, when in town, spent tranquil days, and, amidst the whirl and gaiety of Paris, sighed (he tells us) "twice or thrice a day" for the "arm-chair" and the "retreat" it afforded him.[1] It is a curious fact that the house was for a time rented from Hume by James Boswell, who there received Dr. Samuel Johnson, whose antipathy to its owner was so extreme; and during Hume's absence in France it was occupied by Dr. Blair.

Among the new friendships made by Hume in these years, mention should be made of two of some interest in a controversial respect. In 1761, Hume had submitted to him the sermon of Dr. Campbell, of Aberdeen, afterwards enlarged into the *Dissertation on Miracles*, and, in offering his criticisms, took considerable exception to some of its expressions—particularly one in which he was denominated "an infidel writer." Campbell complaisantly toned down the offensive passages, and an interchange of complimentary letters followed,

[1] Burton, ii. p. 173.

in one of which Hume gives the account, formerly alluded to,[1] of how the Essay on Miracles originated. One paragraph from a letter to Dr. Blair in this connection deserves to be quoted, as showing the terms on which Hume maintained his intimacy with his clerical friends. It is this:—

"Having said so much to your friend [Dr. C.], who is certainly a very ingenious man, though a little too zealous for a philosopher, permit me also the freedom of saying a word to yourself. Whenever I have had the pleasure to be in your company, if the discourse turned upon any common subject of literature, or reasoning, I always parted from you both entertained and instructed. But when the conversation was diverted by you from this channel towards the subject of your profession; though I doubt not but your intentions were very friendly towards me, I own I never received the same satisfaction. I was apt to be tired, and you to be angry. I would therefore wish for the future, whenever my good fortune throws me in your way, that these topics should be foreborne between us. I have long since done with all inquiries on such subjects, and am become incapable of instruction, though I own that no one is more capable of conveying it than yourself."[2]

Two years later (1763) Hume was brought into communication, again through Dr. Blair, with another and more formidable opponent—Dr. Thomas Reid. Reid was at the time preparing his *Inquiry into the Human Mind*, in confutation of Hume's principles. "I wish," said Hume, when he heard of it, "that the parsons would confine themselves to their old occupation of

[1] See above, p. 26. [2] Burton, ii. p. 177.

worrying one another, and leave philosophers to argue with temper, moderation, and good manners"[1]—an observation of which neither the "temper" nor the "good manners" is conspicuous. The perusal of the manuscript changed his opinion, and he wrote to Reid in warm appreciation of the "deeply philosophical" spirit of his work. The reply he received must have more than gratified his vanity, and soothed him for any disappointment he had felt at the earlier neglect of his works. Reid wrote:—

"In attempting to throw some new light upon these abstruse subjects, I wish to preserve the due mean betwixt confidence and despair. But whether I have any success in this attempt or not, I shall always avow myself your disciple in metaphysics. I have learned more from your writings in this kind than from all others put together. Your system appears to me not only coherent in all its parts, but likewise justly deduced from principles commonly received among philosophers; principles which I never thought of calling in question until the conclusions you draw from them in the *Treatise of Human Nature* made me suspect them. If these principles are solid, your system must stand; and whether they are or not, can better be judged after you have brought to light the whole system that grows out of them, than when the greater part of it was wrapped up in clouds and darkness. I agree with you, therefore, that if this system shall ever be demolished, you have a just claim to a great share of the praise, both because you have made it a distinct and determinate aim to be marked at, and have furnished proper artillery for the purpose."[2]

[1] Burton, ii. p. 153. [2] *Ibid.* ii. p. 155.

We now approach what may be termed the crowning triumph of Hume's life—the period of his French visit. Hume made no secret at any time that the French were the people he most admired.[1] He was now to have experience of the extraordinary degree in which they admired him. The new period is led up to by a correspondence opened in 1761 with a lady of accomplishment and high social rank—the Comtesse de Boufflers—who, if we may believe herself, had been transported almost beyond the power of expression by the exquisite qualities of Hume's genius. The fact that this lady held the equivocal position of mistress to the Prince of Conti, seems neither to have occasioned any trouble in her own mind nor excited any disapprobation in that of Hume.[2] In the interchange of letters that followed, Hume and the Comtesse vied with each other in the exuberance of their compliments; and if Hume escaped thinking himself a demi-god, or something very near it, the blame cannot be laid at the door of his fair correspondent. For instance:—

"I know no terms capable of expressing what I felt in reading this work (the *History*). I was moved, transported; and the emotion which it caused in me is, in some measure, painful by its continuance. . . . But how shall I be able to express the effect produced on me by your divine impartiality? I would that I had, on this occasion, your own eloquence in which

[1] Burton, ii. pp. 165, 179, etc.

[2] Her regard for the Prince he considered as "really honourable and virtuous" (Burton, ii. p. 248). He became her confidant, and did his best to console her for her disappointment in not being made Princess at her husband's death.

to express my thought! In truth, I believed I had before my eyes the work of some celestial being, free from the passions of humanity, who, for the benefit of the human race, has deigned to write the events of these latter times."[1]

Madame de Boufflers had heard that Hume had some intention of coming to Paris, and exerted all her powers of persuasion to induce him to do so. She also wrote soliciting his interest on behalf of the exiled J. J. Rousseau, in the event of that persecuted man seeking an asylum in England. We shall see what came of that request afterwards. Meanwhile the way for the visit to Paris was opened up in an unexpected manner. In the middle of 1763, Hume received an invitation from the Marquis of Hertford, Ambassador to the Court of France, to accompany him in the capacity of acting secretary.[2] No offer could be more flattering to Hume, or more agreeable to his inclinations; and its material advantages—the settlement upon him of a pension of £200 for life, with the near prospect of becoming full secretary to the Embassy at £1000 a year—were very great. His first impulse was to decline; but, bethinking himself, as he instructively says, "that I had in a manner abjured all literary occupations; that I resolved to give up my future life entirely to amusements; that there could not be a better pastime than such a journey, especially with a man of Lord Hertford's character,"[3] he decided to accept, and in August 1763

[1] Burton, ii. pp. 95-6.

[2] The official secretary was one Sir Charles Bunbury, an incapable man, whom Hertford refused to have with him.

[3] Burton, ii. p. 158.

set out for London, arriving in Paris with the Embassy on the 14th of October following.

It would be unprofitable to dwell on the details of Hume's residence in France during the next two years, and only general features need be sketched. His welcome in that country exceeded all expectations. Lord Elibank, writing from Paris on 11th May 1763, had said to him: "No author ever yet attained to that degree of reputation in his own lifetime that you are now in possession of at Paris";[1] and Hume found that this statement was no exaggeration. His connection with Hertford opened to him the circles of highest distinction at Court; his literary celebrity was an even surer passport to the brilliant society of the *salons*. On all sides he was fêted, flattered, honoured; was smothered in compliments by the ladies; was extolled among the literati as a genius of transcendent merit. A paragraph or two from his letters will suffice in illustration of his reception at Paris and at Fontainebleau:—

"I have been three days at Paris, and two at Fontainebleau," he says, "and have everywhere met with the most extraordinary honours, which the most exorbitant vanity could wish or desire. The compliments of dukes and marischals of France, and foreign ambassadors, go for nothing with me at present; I retain a relish for no kind of flattery but that which comes from the ladies." (To Adam Smith.)[2]

"I have now passed four days at Paris, and about a fortnight in the Court of Fontainebleau, amidst a people who, from the royal family downwards, seem to have it much at heart to persuade me, by every

[1] Burton, ii. p. 167. [2] *Ibid.* ii. p. 168.

expression of esteem, that they consider me one of the greatest geniuses in the world. I am convinced that Louis XIV. never, in any three weeks of his life, suffered so much flattery; I say suffered, for it really confounds and embarrasses me, and makes me look sheepish." (To Professor Ferguson.)[1]

"Do you ask me about my course of life? I can only say, that I eat nothing but ambrosia, drink nothing but nectar, breathe nothing but incense, and tread on nothing but flowers! Every man I meet, and, still more, every lady, would think they were wanting in the most indispensable duty if they did not make a long and elaborate harangue in my praise." (To Dr. Robertson.)[2]

France—gay, corrupt, and unbelieving—was hastening to its inevitable doom of twenty-five years later; but Hume seems to have had not the remotest inkling of the fact. What he did see was a charmingly cultivated and polite people, wholly possessed by a rage for letters! In the halls of the great, and at the supper-tables of the ladies who presided nightly over their respective coteries of wits and philosophers, Hume soon made the acquaintance of most of the men of distinction of the day—of D'Alembert, Turgot, Helvetius, Marmontel, Buffon, Diderot, and a host of others—and was lionised by all to the top of his bent. It is to the credit of the good sense of Hume that this excess of flattery did not altogether spoil him. It would be foolish to say that it was not agreeable to him; it amused him and gratified his vanity; he could not help contrasting it with the coldness of his reception at home; at the bottom of his mind, perhaps, he

[1] Burton, ii. p. 172. [2] *Ibid.* ii. p. 177.

did not disdain the thought that he deserved it. But his letters give abundant evidence that he did not lose his head over it. He constantly protests that it made little difference to his happiness; that the excess of it palled upon him; that he longed to escape from it to the quiet of his old life.

"I am sensible," he writes to Ferguson, in a passage formerly alluded to, "that I set out too late, and that I am misplaced; and I wish, twice or thrice a day, for my easy-chair and my retreat in James's Court! Never think, dear Ferguson, that as long as you are master of your own fireside and your own time, you can be unhappy, or that any other circumstance can make an addition to your enjoyment."[1]

But this, too, was a mood; and, on the whole, it must be pronounced that Hume thoroughly enjoyed his life at Paris—got so used to it, indeed, that it became a question with him whether he could ever part with it!

Many anecdotes, naturally, cluster round this period when Hume was, as Walpole maliciously called him, the "mode" in fashionable and literary circles in the French capital. Hume himself tells that as society got more familiar with him it found in him a source of some amusement. "They now begin to banter me," he says, "and tell droll stories of me, which they have either observed themselves, or have heard from others."[2] This was inevitable, for neither in personal appearance nor in address could Hume ever be aught but a contrast to the gay, frivolous company in which he mingled. "No lady's toilet," Lord Charlemont sarcastically tells us, "was complete without Hume's

[1] Burton, ii. p. 173. [2] *Ibid.* ii. p. 178.

attendance"; "at the opera his broad unmeaning face was usually seen *entre deux jolis minois.*"[1] It is an amusing picture which Madame d'Epinay has given of his appearance, in his rôle of Sultan, in an acted tableau at a fashionable evening entertainment. Seated on a sofa between two of the loveliest women of Paris, he is supposed to be demonstrating his affections to two slaves, who turn a deaf ear to his protestations. But during a quarter of an hour he can think of nothing better to do than, fixing his gaze upon the beauties, to beat upon his knees and *stomach*, and keep repeating, *Eh bien! mes demoiselles. . . . Eh bien! vous voilà donc. . . . Eh bien! vous voilà . . . vous voilà ici!* One of the ladies at length bounces off in her impatience, exclaiming, *Cet homme n'est bon qu' à manger du veau!* ("This man is only fit to eat veal.")[2]

Of a different stamp is a story told to Sir Samuel Romilly by Diderot of a dinner at Baron d'Holbach's. There was a large company, and the conversation turned on natural religion. "As for atheists," said Hume, "I don't believe that they exist; I never saw one." "You have been a little unfortunate," replied his host; "you are here at table for the first time *with seventeen of them.*"[3]

Hume's position in the Embassy, as already seen, was that of acting secretary, while another (Sir Charles Bunbury) held the title to the office, and drew its emoluments in London. This was manifestly an unfair arrangement, and Hume's patron and Hume himself were alike anxious to have the office and its rewards transferred to the person who really did the

[1] Burton, ii. p. 223. [2] *Ibid.* ii. p. 224.
[3] *Ibid.* ii. p. 229.

work.[1] Hume was concerned also, lest, in the rapid changes of political parties in England, he should find the life-pension that had been promised him suddenly vanishing. In letters to Sir Gilbert Elliot, of Minto, and other acquaintances, he solicits, at Lord Hertford's instigation, their influence on his behalf, though he intimates that he is doubtful of success. The matter, however, happily arranged itself in the end through the transference of Sir Charles Bunbury to the post (for which he was equally unqualified) of Secretary for Ireland, when, by the aid of friends, among whom Madame de Boufflers is to be named, Hume was (June 1765) made secretary to the Embassy, with a salary of £1200 a year. But his ambition in this respect had scarcely been realised when a new change took place. Lord Hertford was recalled to fill the high office of Lord Lieutenant of Ireland, and Hume was left for the time as *chargé d'affaires* in Paris. The duties of that responsible position he discharged with assiduity and ability till near the close of the year. Lord Hertford's original design had been to take Hume with him to Ireland. This he did not accomplish; but he succeeded in obtaining for him the comfortable pension of £400 a year for life. Thus, at the conclusion of his two and a half years' sojourn in Paris, our philosopher was, if not rich, at least in possession of a very substantial income.

A piece of correspondence which belongs to this Parisian period cannot here be passed over, though the light it throws on Hume's principles of conduct is anything but a pleasant one. It is his reply to the letter of Colonel Edmonstone, asking, with regard to a young

[1] Burton, ii. p. 189.

man who was "a sort of a disciple" of Hume's own, whether it would be legitimate for him to take orders as a clergyman of the Church of England. "You'll determine," the writer says, "whether a man of probity can accept of a living, a bishoprick, that does not believe all the Thirty-nine Articles, for you only can fix him: he has been hitherto irresolute." Hume's answer gives us a glimpse into his own mind:—

"It is putting too great a respect on the vulgar, and on their superstitions, to pique oneself on sincerity with regard to them. Did ever any one make it a point of honour to speak the truth to children or madmen? If the thing were worthy being treated gravely, I should tell him, that the Pythian oracle, with the approbation of Xenophon, advised every one to worship the gods—νομῳ πολεως. I wish it were still in my power to be a hypocrite in this particular. The common duties of society usually require it; and the ecclesiastical profession only adds a little more to an innocent dissimulation, or rather simulation, without which it is impossible to pass through the world. Am I a liar, because I order my servant to say, I am not at home, when I do not desire to see company?"[1]

To this, then, Hume's philosophy brings us—deliberate falsehood and hypocrisy in the holiest region of our lives!

The story of this part of Hume's career may be briefly completed. After many fluctuations of purpose as to the place of his abode, he returned to England with Rousseau (of whom more anon), in January 1766. He remained in London till midsummer, then went north to Edinburgh; but had not

[1] Burton, ii. p. 187.

been many months there when he was honoured with a fresh invitation to become Under-Secretary of State for Scotland (there being at the time no principal Secretary). Early in 1767, accordingly, we find him again in London, installed in this secretarial office, whose duties he continued to discharge till 20th July 1768. In the following year he came back to Edinburgh, re-establishing himself in his domicile in James's Court. His own account is: "I returned to Edinburgh in 1769, very opulent (for I possessed a revenue of £1000 a year), and though somewhat stricken in years [he was fifty-eight years of age], with the prospect of enjoying long my ease, and of seeing the increase of my reputation." Strange how this note of his "reputation" is invariably the dominant one!

A little must now be said of an episode which perhaps stirred Hume more deeply than any other experience in his life: his famous quarrel with the eccentric and only half responsible Swiss genius and sentimentalist, Jean Jacques Rousseau. There is nothing in this episode but what redounds to Hume's credit and kindness of heart; but it reveals, what other instances also discover,[1] how much passion, and vehemence of resentment, when his *amour propre* was touched,

[1] His biographer remarks on an earlier correspondence (with Lord Elibank), that "it shows that he was by no means exempt from the passion of anger, and that when under its influence he was liable to be harsh and unreasonable," and refutes "the general notion formed of his character," viz., "that he passed through life unmoved and immovable, a placid mass of breathing flesh, on which the ordinary impulses which rouse the human passions into life might expend themselves in vain" (ii. p. 251). Hume, in fact, could be aroused to an astonishing strength of indignation, when either his person or opinions received what he regarded as injustice. Cf. pp. 15, 39.

lurked beneath our philosopher's ordinarily placid demeanour. Reference was made above to a letter of the Comtesse de Boufflers in 1762, recommending Rousseau to Hume's good offices, should he come to England. Letters from the exiled Earl Marischal of Scotland, then Governor of Neufchâtel, bore on the same subject.[1] The facts, briefly, were that Rousseau, who had been living peacefully at Montmorency under the protection of his friends the Duke and Duchess of Luxembourg, had been compelled in 1762, by the storm of persecution which broke out on the publication of his *Emile*, to flee the kingdom of France, and take refuge in Switzerland. He found an asylum at Neufchâtel, then under Prussian sovereignty; but his friends thought it wiser that he should seek refuge in England. Hume warmly interested himself in the project, assuring Madame de Boufflers that "there is no man in Europe of whom I have entertained a higher idea, and whom I would be prouder to serve."[2] Rousseau's pride, however, prevented him from receiving the proffered favours; and he continued to reside at various retreats in Switzerland, persecuted by priests and populace, and made miserable by his own self-tormenting disposition, until October 1765, when he left for Strassburg, and, in December, at Hume's invitation,[3] found his way to Paris. In all these wanderings he was accompanied by his coarse-natured mistress, Thérèse le Vasseur. With genuine goodness of heart, Hume took him in hand, had him provided for by the Prince of Conti, and, as we have seen, brought him with himself to England in January 1766.

[1] Burton, ii. pp. 102–110.
[2] *Ibid.* ii. p. 108.
[3] *Ibid.* ii. p. 309.

He could not be unobservant of Rousseau's peculiar humours, but then and for months afterwards, he entertained the highest opinion of the strange being with whose fame Europe at the time was ringing. "My companion," he writes on 19th January, "is very amiable, always polite, gay often, commonly sociable.... I love him very much, and hope that I may have some share in his affections."[1] And on 2nd February, "He is a very modest, mild, well-bred, gentle-spirited, and warm-hearted man, as ever I knew in my life. He is also to appearance very sociable. I never saw a man who seems better calculated for good company, nor who seems to take more pleasure in it."[2] Hume kept him at his house in London, obtained for him from the King the promise of a pension of £100 a year, and, not to delay on other kindnesses, as Rousseau seemed bent on a life of solitude, finally arranged for his being established in the charmingly situated country mansion of Wooton, in Derbyshire, the property of a Mr. Davenport, who took a warm interest in the fortunes of the wanderer. To soothe Rousseau's susceptibilities, Mr. Davenport agreed to accept £30 a year for board!

All this, however, was in vain, so far as the securing of Rousseau's happiness was concerned. It was the misfortune of this singularly-constituted individual, that, as one has said, he had an "utter incapacity for establishing healthy relations with one single human being";[3] and his morbid sensibility, egoistic jealousy, and passionate craving for a notoriety which he continually affected to denounce, made him the victim

[1] Burton, ii. p. 303. [2] *Ibid.* ii. p. 309.

[3] Caird's *Essays on Literature and Philosophy* ("Rousseau"), i. p. 107.

of perpetual suspicions and delusions. He coquetted with the proposed pension from the King, and appeared to refuse it; then, in answer to a letter of Hume on the subject, amazed that philosopher by an epistle (23rd June) in which he flatly accused Hume of being engaged, all the while he was professing friendship, of deep designs against his honour, and broke off further correspondence with him. Hume replied in not unnatural heat, demanding an explanation of these extraordinary charges. This elicited, in three weeks' time, an "enormous" letter—thirty-five pages of print —in which Rousseau, in the form of a continuous narrative, piles up, with no better a foundation than his own diseased imaginations, the supposed proofs of Hume's wicked conspiracies against him since their relations began. It would be profitless to enter into the details of charges so ridiculous. The occasion of the whole was a silly satire on Rousseau which Sir Robert Walpole had set abroad in Paris in form of a letter from Frederick of Prussia, by which Rousseau's vanity was deeply wounded. He at first thought the insult was by Voltaire; when he discovered Walpole's share in the jest, he immediately suspected Hume of being privy to it. This suspicion once planted in his mind, he found confirmations of it in every word, act, and look of Hume's—even those in which Hume was most his friend. Hume was not less shocked at the discovery he supposed he had made of the baseness and ingratitude of one for whom he had done so much; and, not content with repelling Rousseau's own attacks, wrote freely on the subject to his friends in Scotland and France. He declares to Blair that Rousseau is "surely the blackest and most atrocious villain, beyond comparison, that now exists in the world, and I am heartily ashamed of anything I ever wrote in his favour."[1] His letters to Baron d'Holbach, to D'Alembert, to Madame de Boufflers, and others in Paris, are couched in the same indignant and vindicatory strain. "Surely," he says to the Abbé Le Blanc, "never was there so much wickedness and madness combined in one human creature."[2] In all this Hume did not exhibit his usual self-restraint. He was even moved, though Rousseau had published nothing, to give to the world an *exposé* of the whole quarrel, and this, with accompanying documents, was published, first in French, then in English. It need only be added that in April 1767 Rousseau voluntarily fled with Mademoiselle le Vasseur from his retreat at Wooton, leaving about £30, with his baggage, in Mr. Davenport's possession. He betook himself to Paris, where he had an unfriendly reception;[3] and he seems afterwards to have regretted his foolish behaviour. Hume also is known to have exerted himself in 1767 to protect him from the French Government. We gather from a letter of Mr. Davenport's that Rousseau's pension was continued to him.[4] This gentleman's kind forbearance to the unhappy exile is one of the relieving features of a sordid story.

The short remaining period of Hume's life—the quiet evening of his days—was spent in Edinburgh with scarcely any stronger excitement than that afforded by literary occupations and the society of congenial

[1] Burton, ii. p. 344. [2] *Ibid.* ii. p. 347. [3] *Ibid.* ii. p. 377.

[4] *Ibid.* ii. p. 368. The full account of this dispute may be read in Burton, with whose narrative should be compared Mr. Morley's in his *Rousseau*, vol. ii. ch. vi. Hume's published account of the controversy, with the letters, should also be consulted. It is printed in the Introduction to Hume's Works (1854), vol. i.

friends. In 1771 the house in James's Court was exchanged for one more suitable to his enlarged means, built at the corner of what is now St. David Street, in the new part of the city. The name of the street originated, it is well known, from the wit of a young lady, who chalked the words on the walls of Hume's habitation. Hume took the jest in good part, remarking to the servant-girl who ran in, much excited, to tell him what had been done, "Never mind, lassie, many a better man has been made a saint of before!"[1] The desire for further travel or change seems absolutely to have deserted him once he was ensconced in his old quarters. "I have been settled here two months," he writes in 1769, "and am here body and soul, without casting the least thought of regret to London, or even to Paris."[2] The English he had always cordially disliked, and his feelings towards them in these last years seemed to acquire a character of ever-deepening antipathy. What repelled him was the scorn and contempt of the English for the Scots and for things Scotch. He had written earlier (1765) to Millar (one of many similar ebullitions): "The rage and prejudice of parties frighten me; above all, this rage against the Scots, which is so dishonourable, and indeed so infamous to the English nation. We hear that it increases every day without the least appearance of provocation on our part."[3] Now we find him denouncing to Sir Gilbert Elliot "the daily and hourly progress of madness, and folly, and wickedness in England,"[4] and declaring, "Our Government has become a chimera, and is too perfect, in point of liberty, for so rude a

[1] Burton, ii. p. 436.
[2] *Ibid.* ii. p. 431.
[3] *Ibid.* ii. p. 265.
[4] *Ibid.* ii. p. 431.

beast as an Englishman; who is a man, a bad animal too, corrupted by above a century of licentiousness."[1] The only literary work in which he indulged himself, besides correspondence, was the continued revision of his former works. And this, again, as regards the *History*, meant chiefly, as we saw, the purging out of remaining traces of Whiggism. Thus, to Elliot: "I am running over again the last edition of my *History*, in order to correct it still further. I either soften or expunge many villainous, seditious Whig strokes, which had crept into it. . . . I am sensible that the first editions were too full of those foolish English prejudices, which all nations and all ages disavow."[2]

The social life of Edinburgh in which Hume participated was such as had many charms for a man of his genial disposition, and literary and philosophic tastes. His habits were simple, and his circumstances sufficiently affluent to raise him above all worldly cares. He had obtained the fame which was his chief object in life, and he was welcomed as visitor or friend in the best society. His intimate associates were men of liberal, cultivated mind; and the conversation at the supper-table, in the philosophical gathering, or at the more convivial club, was sure to be enlivened by abundance of anecdote, witty repartee, or criticism of what was newest in politics or letters. Free from the faintest taint of religious feeling himself, he had no sympathy with "fanaticism" and "enthusiasm" in others, and could rely on finding this element abso-

[1] Burton, ii. p. 434.

[2] *Ibid.* With all his desire and labour to clear his writings from Scotticisms, it is characteristic that he preserved to the last his broad Doric in conversation.

lutely excluded from the eminently "rational" circles in which he moved. With a Blair and a Robertson it was a condition of his intercourse that the subject of religion should not be obtruded.[1] With more jovial spirits like Carlyle, of Inveresk, he could have little fear that it would ever be introduced, save by way of jest. In the calm, philosophic heights to which it was relegated by a Ferguson or an Adam Smith, it could not affect him much either one way or another. Yet it is the testimony of every one who knew him, that Hume never wantonly or inconsiderately wounded the religious susceptibilities of others by untimely airing of his own sceptical opinions. His amiable social qualities, on the other hand, are universally extolled. He was, his friends unite in telling us, simple, natural, and playful; unaffected in manner, and kindly in disposition; charitable to those in need; pleasing and instructive in his conversation alike to young and old. His mother's epithet "good-natured" clung to him to the last, whatever might be said of the "wake-mindedness." His own description of his character in his *Life* is, it will perhaps be felt, as good as any:—

"I was, I say, a man of mild disposition, of command of temper, of an open, social, and cheerful humour, capable of attachment, but little susceptible of enmity, and of great moderation in all my passions. Even my love of literary fame, my ruling passion, never soured my temper, notwithstanding my frequent disappointments. My company was not unacceptable to the young and careless, as well as to the studious and literary; and as I took a particular pleasure in the company of modest women, I had no reason to be

[1] See above, p. 62.

displeased with the reception I met with from them."

Yet in the whole picture which Hume draws of himself, it is remarkable that he does not acknowledge, or hint at, a single fault. The sketch is self-complacency throughout.

The letters of this closing period would seem to indicate that in his last years Hume's thought and conversation turned a good deal on politics, and that his wide connection with public men and public affairs furnished him with a store of anecdote and reminiscence on which he was never unwilling to draw. It is worth observing that, with all his Tory leanings, Hume was from the first opposed to the American War, and foresaw its disastrous results. His views are indicated in various letters, but may perhaps best be inferred *per oppositum* from the following letter, in reply to one of his, from Mr. Strahan, his printer, which is in its own way a gem—of unwisdom. Mr. Strahan says:—

"I differ from you *toto cœlo* with regard to America. I am entirely for coercive methods with those obstinate madmen; and why should we despair of success? Why should we suffer the empire to be so dismembered, without the utmost exertions on our part? I see nothing so very formidable in this business, if we become a little more unanimous, and could stop the mouths of domestic traitors, from whence the evil originated. Not that I wish to enslave the colonists, or to make them one jot less happy than ourselves; but I am for keeping them subordinate to the British Legislature; and their trade, to a reasonable degree, subservient to the interest of the mother country; but which she must inevitably lose, if they are emancipated, as you propose. I am very surprised you are of a different opinion. Very true, things look oddly at present; and the dispute hath, hitherto, been very ill managed; but so we always do at the commencement of every war. So we did most remarkably in the last. . . . But, so soon as the British lion is roused, we never fail to fetch up our leeway, as the sailors say. And so I hope you will find it in this important case."[1]

In the spring of 1775, Hume experienced the first symptoms of that internal disorder—a hæmorrhage of the bowels—which had its fatal termination in the course of the following year. At first the distemper created little alarm, but its persistence and increasing gravity soon marked it as likely to be incurable. By the commencement of 1776, Hume found that he had fallen off "five complete stones" in weight.[2] His cheerfulness continued unabated, and his letters to Gibbon and Adam Smith show the lively interest excited in his mind by the publication of *The Decline and Fall* of the one, and *The Wealth of Nations* of the other.[3] The serious state of his health led him, on 4th January, to execute a settlement, in which, besides the provisions for the disposal of his estate, he made careful arrangement for the publication of his *Dialogues on Natural Religion*, hitherto, by the urgency of his friends, withheld from the press. The bulk of his fortune he left to his brother, and after him to his nephew David; his sister was to receive £1200; among his legacies was one to D'Alembert of £200, and another of the

[1] Burton, ii. p. 477. Probably Hume's French connection influenced his views.

[2] *Ibid.* ii. p. 483.

[3] *Ibid.* ii. pp. 484–7.

same sum to Adam Ferguson. Adam Smith was appointed his literary executor, and on him was laid the injunction of publishing the formidable *Dialogues.* Difficulties, however, arose on this point. Dr. Blair, Sir Gilbert Elliot, and Smith himself, were strongly opposed to the publication of this work, which struck, as they regarded it, at the foundations of Theism; and the last must have plainly indicated to Hume his unwillingness to take the responsibility laid upon him. Hume was as firmly resolved that the *Dialogues* should see the light; and while, in a qualifying letter to Smith of 3rd May, he left it to his discretion to publish or not as he saw fit, he soon after, in a codicil to his will (7th August), altered the disposition he had made, and left his manuscripts to the care of Mr. William Strahan, "trusting to the friendship that has long subsisted between us, for his careful and faithful execution of my intentions." He desired that the *Dialogues* might be printed and published any time within two years after his death; and, failing this, he ordained that the property should return to his nephew David, "whose duty, in publishing them, as the last request of his uncle, must be approved by all the world."[1] In point of fact, the duty was declined by Strahan, as by the others; and the *Dialogues* were only at length published, in accordance with Hume's wishes, by his nephew in 1779. In April 1776, Hume wrote the sketch of his own life which has been frequently referred to, and directions were left that it should be prefixed to any future edition of his works.

The end was now drawing sensibly near. A journey which Hume undertook in April and May, at the desire

[1] Burton, ii. pp. 493–4.

of his friends, to London and Bath, though marked by gleams of hope, failed of any lasting good effect, and in the beginning of June he returned to Edinburgh, consciously to take leave of his friends and of the world. The prospect filled him with no alarm. If he cherished no religious hopes, it must be confessed that he had schooled his mind into a scepticism which seemed to enable him to dispense with them. He spoke of his approaching end with calmness and even playfulness; he maintained his usual unaffected cheerfulness in company; he uttered no repining at a departure which, he reasoned, only cut off a few years of infirmities. In his own last words in his *Life*, one finds the old note of his literary reputation still uppermost. "Though I see," he says, "many symptoms of my literary reputation's breaking out at last with additional lustre, I knew that I could have but few years to enjoy it." His friends, who were unremitting in their devotion to him, overflow in their admiration and astonishment at the composure, the imperturbability, the cheerfulness, the gaiety even,—as in his jesting about Charon and his boat,[1]—with which he met the dread event of death, to most so sad and solemn. He is to them the very ideal of the sage. And so, indeed, he would be, if the foundations on which his philosophic indifference rested were sound,—if human life had, indeed, no higher meaning, no weightier responsibilities, no more earnest purpose, no more awful issues, than he supposed. But that "if" makes all the difference in our sense of the fitness of things in the way of quitting life.

Hume died on the Sunday, 25th August 1776, "in

[1] Burton, ii. p. 511.

such a happy composure of mind," says his physician, "that nothing could exceed it."[1] He was buried, amidst abundant manifestations of the public interest, friendly and hostile, evoked by his person and opinions, in the old graveyard on Calton Hill, then in the open country; and above his remains was reared the circular monument still to be seen, on which is inscribed, by his express directions, only the simple words, "David Hume," with the years of his birth and death—"leaving it," as he significantly says in his will, "to posterity to add the rest."

[1] Burton, ii. p. 511.

CHAPTER V

HUME IN RELATION TO PREVIOUS PHILOSOPHY—HIS SCEPTICISM

IT is chiefly in connection with his speculations in philosophy and morals that Hume's name will go down to posterity. In other walks of literature he holds a high and honourable, but by no means a peculiar place. He is *unus ex multis*—no more. Even as a historian his fame in later years has been eclipsed by that of abler, and more learned and impartial writers. But as philosopher his speculations have passed into universal thought. Here his niche is his own. There is but one Hume, as there is but one Descartes and one Kant.

It has been seen that Hume's first and greatest philosophical work was his celebrated *Treatise of Human Nature*, published anonymously in 1739–40, and that the chief portion of this work was afterwards recast, and published in more compact and literary form, in the *Enquiry concerning the Human Understanding*, in 1748. The roots of his system, however, are all to be sought for in the *Treatise*.

The aim of both of these works is avowedly to inquire into the nature, operations, and limits of the human mind. The different parts of this inquiry, held to be the grand prerequisite to success in all other departments of human knowledge, are stated with great distinctness in the introductory section of the *Enquiry* on "The Different Species of Philosophy."[1] There is first psychology, or, as Hume terms it, "the geography of the mental faculties." Here, at least, he admits, we are on solid ground.[2] The next inquiry is a deeper one. "May we not hope," he says, "that philosophy, if cultivated with care, may carry its researches still further, and discover, at least in some degree, the secret springs and principles by which the human mind is actuated in its operations."[3] The purpose of his investigation, therefore, is to disclose the ultimate principle or principles of intelligence—to run up all the operations of the mind to some principle which is "general and universal."[4] As yet there is no hint given of his peculiar scepticism; on the contrary, though the investigation is owned to be a difficult one, his tone is courageous and hopeful. He chooses to start with the usual assumption that truth is within our reach, leaving it to his after reasonings to disprove the postulate. It is only as the system advances that we begin to see whither we are drifting. It will facilitate the understanding of Hume's positions, and especially of his scepticism, if, before entering on the details of his system, we look shortly at the antecedents of his thinking in Locke and Berkeley, the philosophers by whom he was most influenced. We shall then consider more precisely the nature of the scepticism itself.

[1] With Hume's remarks in this section may be compared Locke's "Epistle to the Reader," prefixed to this *Essay*, and the Preface to a still greater work—Kant's *Kritik*.

[2] Works, iv. p. 10. [3] *Ibid.* p. 12. [4] *Ibid.*

Philosophy may be described in general as the study of the nature of knowledge, and, through that, of the nature of reality as given in our experience. There are two main questions in the present connection:—

1*st.* How do we know the external world, all knowledge (ideas) being in the mind, while objects are *ex hypothesi* out of and separate from the mind?

2*nd.* Is all our knowledge derived from experience, or does any of it spring from the nature of the thinking faculty, or from reason?

The ambiguity of this second mode of stating the question will appear after. The real question will be found to be, what *is* experience? Is sense the whole, or is there a rational factor involved in the constitution of even the simplest experience? It was, however, in the assumption underlying the first question that Hume and the philosophers who preceded him found their common ground. Whatever differences divided Descartes and Locke on such a subject as "innate ideas," they were at one in the fundamental point that the sole object of the mind's knowledge *is its own ideas.* This was regarded by all thinkers as so self-evident as to need no proof. "It is universally allowed by philosophers," says Hume, "and is besides pretty obvious of itself, that nothing is ever really present with the mind but its perceptions or impressions and ideas, and that external objects become known to us only by those perceptions they occasion."[1] From the admission of this position, it has commonly been attempted to show that the whole of Hume's conclusions follow by inevitable sequence. This, we shall see, is only in part correct. The statement is strictly true

[1] Works, i. p. 93.

only of the Lockean or empirical variety of the theory of ideas. Kant, *e.g.*, is as subjective as Hume in the assertion that objects are only known to us through the impressions they excite in us, but his theory involves rational elements which save knowledge from the utter disintegration it undergoes at the hands of Hume. It is in the line of the empirical development of philosophy, however, that Hume stands. Hence it is sufficient to trace the genealogy of his views, as proposed, from Locke and Berkeley.[1]

The answer given by Locke to the question of the origin of knowledge was on lines which the average intelligence of mankind would regard as those of plain common sense. He rejects the hypothesis of innate ideas. The mind has no ideas but those which it derives from experience, and, in the first instance, through the gateways of the senses. Prior to sensible experience, the mind is a *tabula rasa*, a "white paper, void of all characters, without any ideas,"[2] an "empty cabinet," waiting to be furnished with ideas "let in" by the senses.[3] Knowledge begins with the impressions produced by the outward world on the organs of sense. These, conveyed to the brain, give rise to sensations. Thus originate "ideas of sensation," which are the first kind of "simple ideas." Through sensation the mind receives ideas of the qualities of the things which affect it from without—through sight, *e.g.*, ideas of form and colour; through touch, ideas of hardness, softness, roughness, extension, solidity;

[1] Hegel says: "Hume's philosophy starts immediately from the standpoint of Bacon and Locke, which derives our ideas from experience, and his scepticism has the Berkeleian idealism as its basis" (*Geschichte d. Philosophie*, iii. p. 446).

[2] *Essay*, bk. ii. ch. i.

[3] *Ibid.* bk. i. ch. ii.

through hearing, idea of sounds, etc. But, next, the mind can *reflect* on its own operations in dealing with this first class of ideas, as in perception, memory, imagination, reasoning, and on the affections and emotions to which they give rise; and this furnishes it with a second class of ideas, distinguished from the former as "ideas of reflection." "Simple ideas" of both kinds yield through combination "complex ideas," etc. From the ideas derived from these two sources—sensation and reflection—all our knowledge, he contends, is, in the last analysis, built up."[1]

There is another distinction to be observed in regard to these "ideas of sensation," from which, according to Locke, our knowledge of the external world is derived. They fall, he explains, into two classes. The one class of ideas are properly only *effects* produced in us by the operation of external objects, and the idea bears no resemblance to the quality or property in the object which produces it. Such, *e.g.*, are the ideas of sweetness, of warmth, of sound, of colour, which exist only in the mind, and have no resemblance to the physical properties which are their causes. Ideas thus produced in us by properties of body which they in no wise resemble, are called by Locke "ideas of *secondary* qualities." It is different with the other class of ideas. These, it is held, do resemble, are in a manner "copies" or pictures of, the qualities in the object. Thus, the ideas of shape, of figure, of solidity, are produced in us, as before, by the operation of the object; but, unlike the ideas of the secondary qualities,

[1] *Essay*, bk. ii. chs. i., xxiii., xxiv. Certain ideas, as those of existence, power, succession, are supposed to be derived from both sources (bk. ii. ch. vi.).

they have their counterparts in actual qualities of the object, which they resemble. These ideas which have qualities in bodies corresponding to them Locke names "ideas of *primary* qualities." The qualities in bodies themselves are similarly distinguished.

This eminently common-sense account of the origin of our knowledge, however, proves much less satisfactory on closer inspection. The theory bristles, in fact, as the slightest touch of criticism shows, with inconsequences. On the one hand, Locke lays down the doctrine that the mind has knowledge only of its own ideas; while, to account for these ideas he assumes a world of objects lying beyond consciousness, of which the world within our minds is so far a representation. But what is the warrant for this assumption? How can an idea which, *ex hypothesi*, is wholly *within* the mind, yield us the knowledge of an *object* without the mind, or tell us anything of its nature? It is declared that the ideas of "primary" qualities are copies of qualities in the objects. But how is this to be ascertained? Who can overleap his own consciousness to verify the supposed resemblance? If reliance is placed on the principle of causation, it is easy to retort, as was done by both Berkeley and Hume, (1) that causation gives us no title to infer resemblance in the case of "primary" any more than of "secondary" qualities; and (2) that it does not entitle us to infer a material cause—the cause may be *spiritual*.[1] Hume adds to this criticism (3) that the whole procedure is illegitimate, as going beyond experience. "As no beings," he says, "are ever present to the mind but perceptions, it follows that we may observe a conjunction or relation

[1] Works, iv. pp. 174–6.

of cause and effect between different perceptions, but can never observe it between perceptions and objects. It is impossible, therefore, that from the evidence of any of the qualities of the former, we can ever form any conclusion concerning the existence of the latter, or ever satisfy our reason in this particular."[1]

The difficulty, on Locke's theory, is accentuated by the fact that the knowledge we have of the external world is supposed to be derived wholly from sensation. It will be seen later that sensation, as a mode of pure feeling, can give us no idea of objects, or of anything beyond its own immediate existence. But even conceding that, through sensation, we have the idea of external qualities, we are only at the beginning of our difficulties. Qualities, as Locke admits when he comes to deal with that subject,[2] do not subsist of themselves. They are "modes," and modes, he tells us, are necessarily thought of as inhering in "substances." The qualities are qualities of "something." But how are we to represent to ourselves this something, this substance, this substratum of qualities, which, after all, is the real *being* of the thing? It is not an idea of sensation; as little is it an idea of reflection. Whence, then, is it obtained? On Locke's principles there is no room for it at all. No idea, therefore, gave him more trouble. He could neither admit it, nor do without it. He could only reiterate that we must *suppose* a substratum of qualities, though our idea of it is quite "obscure." Locke is in equal difficulties when he passes to the idea of self—the abiding subject of the mental states. That self exists and abides he has no manner of doubt; but whence the idea comes

[1] Works, i. p. 266.

[2] *Essay*, bk. ii. ch. xii.

he has no means of showing. It is not an idea of sense; it is not an idea of a mental operation; whence, then, do we obtain it? It would be easy to show that the theory equally breaks down in the attempt to account for many other ideas; ideas, *e.g.*, of space, time, power, cause, infinity. Such ideas can only be got out of sense if they are first of all surreptitiously put into it.

Berkeley, who followed Locke, had an easy task in disposing of some of these assumptions of his predecessor — especially of that of material substance. Starting from Locke's premiss that the immediate objects of all knowledge are ideas, he pointed out, with perfect logical conclusiveness, that the assumption of a second world of variously-qualified things, outside of and behind the world we know, is entirely without justification. How, indeed, he argued, can ideas of the mind be copies of qualities of objects which we suppose to subsist apart from, and independently of, mind? Is it not the very nature of an idea that it exists only in being perceived? "Their *esse* is *percipi*, nor is it possible they should have any existence out of the minds or thinking things that perceive them."[1] Especially does Berkeley direct his artillery against the Lockean assumption of "substance." Locke had himself admitted that we have no proper idea of this mysterious something, which is made known to us neither by sensation nor by reflection. Berkeley, therefore, justly enough on his premises, swept away these imaginary substances, and with them the world of independently existing objects, and boldly declared that the ideas we perceive by the senses are all the world there is. What

[1] *Principles of Human Knowledge*, pt. i. ch. iii.

we are entitled to infer from their presence is, not that there is, or can be, a world of permanent objects, of which our ideas are images, but that our ideas must have some adequate spiritual cause, and this Berkeley finds in the will of God, who ordains the system of the world in the sense that he causes the ideas to appear in regular series, and in the orderly connection which we call "laws of nature." Hume's criticism on this theory (or class of theory) in turn is:—

"It is too bold ever to carry conviction with it to a man sufficiently apprised of the weakness of human reason. Though the chain of arguments which conduct to it were ever so logical, there must arise a strong suspicion, if not an absolute assurance, that it has carried us quite beyond the reach of our faculties, when it leads to conclusions so extraordinary, and so remote from common life and experience. We are got into fairyland long ere we have reached the last steps of our theory; and *there* we have no reason to trust our common methods of argument."[1]

As if Hume's own reasonings did not conduct to conclusions "extraordinary and remote from common life and experience"!

With regard to mind, on the other hand, Berkeley was plainly in a dilemma. Having, on Locke's principles, discarded "substance" in the sensible world, it was not obvious how he could with consistency retain it in the world of mind. If, however, he could dispense with matter, he as plainly could not dispense with mind as a receptacle of his ideas; and, accordingly, at this point he was compelled to take a step which Locke's principles would not justify. This was to

[1] Works, iv. p. 82.

concede what he calls, not an "idea," but a "notion," of a self as the permanent subject of mental acts and states. When, in his *Principles of Human Knowledge*, he extends this mode of knowledge by means of "notions" to relations, he seems on the verge of breaking away from Locke's principles altogether.

It is now easy, perhaps, to see in a general way how Hume got his starting-point, and was led to his main conclusions. He adopts—we must believe in good faith—the principles of Locke and Berkeley, and draws them out to their ultimate conclusions. Like these philosophers, he takes it for granted as self-evident that the mind has nothing to work on in knowledge but its own ideas, or, as he prefers to call them, "perceptions." The details of his system will occupy us after; meanwhile it is not difficult to forecast what kind of consequences were bound to follow from his stringent logical procedure. The idea of "substance" of course goes. Berkeley had already banished it from the material world, and Hume as summarily dismisses it from the world of mind. The bond of identity is cut, and all existence, inner and outer, is resolved into a train of "impressions and ideas," originating we know not how, and representing nothing but themselves. Objective reality, as we have been accustomed to conceive of it, disappears. There is no self, no external world, no God,[1]—nothing but this stream of perishable "perceptions." Still the irresistible conviction of mankind in the existence of the world and self remains as a fact to be accounted for. Here begins Hume's constructive task, which he

[1] That is, not logically on Hume's premises. On his concessions to Theism, see below, Chapter X.

seeks to accomplish by showing how association and custom create a species of union among our ideas which we mistake for an objective one. The real bearing of all this will be better understood when we have examined, as we now proceed to do, the precise nature of Hume's scepticism.

Philosophy with Hume, as ere long becomes apparent, resolves itself into scepticism. His earliest and most original work represents a vigorous and unsparing attack upon the very foundations of our intelligence, the only object of which seems to be to subvert all rational certainty, and, as Dugald Stewart expressed it, "to produce in the reader a complete distrust of his own faculties."[1] His scepticism was more thorough and systematic than that of any who had preceded him. The "doubt" of Descartes was only prized as it led to a higher certainty, and the same might be said of the scepticism of Pascal. Hume, on the other hand, never sought to go beyond his doubts, but spent his strength in reducing them to scientific form. Even his professed solutions are avowedly "sceptical."[2] Bayle had preceded him in the attempt to establish universal scepticism, availing himself for this purpose of the contradictory opinions of different sects, and skilfully attacking the grounds on which special dogmas were assumed to rest. But Hume, to use his own words, "marched up directly to the capital and centre of the sciences—to human nature itself"[3]—and sought by capturing that to secure an easy victory. He labours to divide the mind against itself, and, by involving it in inextricable self-contradictions, to shake the ground of all its certitude. There are, however, certain peculi-

[1] *Dissertation*, p. 209. [2] *Enquiry*, sec. 5. [3] Works, i. p. 8.

arities of this scepticism of Hume which it will be necessary to examine with greater care; the more that its exact nature has been made the subject of considerable discussion.

One question which has been raised is—Did Hume really accept the conclusions of his own system? The late J. S. Mill, for example, in his *Examination of Hamilton,* broached the peculiar view that Hume's scepticism was simply a thin disguise thrown over his real convictions, intended rather to avoid offence than to conceal his own opinion. "He preferred to be called a sceptic rather than by a more odious name, and having to promulgate conclusions which he knew would be regarded as contradictory, on the one hand, to the evidence of common sense, on the other, to the doctrines of religion, did not like to declare them as positive convictions, but thought it more judicious to exhibit them as the results we might come to, if we put complete confidence in the trustworthiness of our rational faculties."[1] This view of Mill's is opposed to that of Sir William Hamilton, who had represented Hume as reasoning from premises "not established by himself," but "accepted only as principles universally conceded in the previous schools of philosophy."[2] Mr. Mill's judgment is "that Hume seriously accepted both the premises and the conclusions."[3] A narrower inspection may convince us that the truth upon the subject does not lie exclusively with either side.

There can be no doubt that, whatever may have been Hume's real opinions, his avowed sentiments were those of a sceptic, and his reasonings lay all in that

[1] *Exam. of Ham.* p. 555. [2] *Discussions*, pp. 87, 89.
[3] Appendix to *Treatise* (1740).

direction. He was always ready to "plead the privilege of a sceptic,"[1] and no doubt correctly interpreted his own state of mind when he wrote: "A true sceptic will be diffident of his philosophical doubts, as well as of his philosophical convictions."[2] On the other hand, it must be conceded to Mr. Mill's view, that, so far as Hume could allow himself to attain to certainty about anything, he was perfectly serious both in his philosophical starting-point, and in the main conclusions to which his reasonings conducted him. He was playing neither with himself nor with his reader. It is thus, he would hold, we must think, if we are to think philosophically at all. It is difficult to doubt his sincerity in his acceptance of his fundamental position that the mind has nothing present to it but its own "perceptions"; or his *bona fides* in the use he makes of his grand canon, that every idea must be the copy of a previous impression. He would admit that the same certainty does not attach to all his hypotheses in accounting for the particular beliefs of men; but on the whole he is satisfied with the explanations he gives; is sure, at any rate, that if it is not quite thus, it is *somehow* thus, that the thing has come about. We may safely assume that his conviction was as entire as in such a mind it could be, that there is no necessary connection between cause and effect, no substantiality in self or things, no external world apart from our perceptions, no principle stronger than association connecting our ideas.[3]

[1] Appendix to *Treatise* (1740).

[2] Works, i. p. 376.

[3] The most important qualification of this statement is in a passage in the Appendix to his *Treatise* in 1740, in which, while declaring that

There is not, however, the inconsistency which might be supposed between this appearance of certainty in Hume's convictions and the statements formerly made as to his scepticism. The true explanation, as was previously pointed out, undoubtedly is, that Hume's reasonings, pushed to their issues, had a yet more fatal effect than the overthrow of the beliefs of ordinary common sense; they destroyed the authority of reason itself. Mr. Mill had a difficulty in understanding how Hume, if really a sceptic, could reason so seriously and accurately throughout the course of his main discussions. Does not this, he held, imply a certain faith in the operation of "the rational faculty"? He overlooked that, if Hume's premises and conclusions are accepted, there is no "rational faculty" left for us to have faith in. In the last result, reason—or what we call such—destroys its own claim to credit. There is no rational self; no rational instrument which self employs; only combinations of impressions and ideas engendered through association and custom.[1] If it is still argued that this is incompatible with the evident earnestness which Hume shows in reasoning out his conclusions, the answer is furnished by Hume himself. In the *Treatise of Human Nature* he has expressly met this objection, and as the passage casts perhaps a stronger light on the real spirit of that book than any other, we make no apology for quoting it:—

"If the sceptical reasonings be strong, they say, 'tis

he can find no flaw in his reasonings, he confesses his difficulty on the subject of Personal Identity.

[1] See his *Treatise*, pt. iv., "Of Scepticism with regard to Reason," and "Of Scepticism with regard to the Senses"; and the *Enquiry*, sec. 12, "Of the Academic or Sceptical Philosophy."

a proof that reason may have some force and authority; if weak, they can never be sufficient to invalidate all the conclusions of our understanding. The argument is not just. . . . Reason first appears in possession of the throne, prescribing laws, and imposing maxims, with an absolute sway and authority. Her enemy, therefore, is obliged to take shelter under her protection, and by making use of rational arguments to prove the fallaciousness and imbecility of reason produces in a manner a patent under her own hand and seal. This patent has at first an authority proportioned to the present and immediate authority of reason, from which it is derived. But as it is supposed contradictory to reason, it gradually diminishes the force of the governing power, and its own at the same time; till at last they both vanish away into nothing by a regular and just diminution."[1]

It requires considerable faith after this to believe that Hume "put complete confidence in the trustworthiness of our rational faculty," as Mr. Mill "has little doubt that he did."[2] Mr. Mill is certainly in error when he affirms that any intimations to the contrary are found only "in a few detached passages" in a single essay—that "On the Academical or Sceptical Philosophy."[3] The *Treatise of Human Nature* abounds with them. In the *Enquiry*, no doubt, in harmony with the *moral* purpose of his philosophy—to clear the way for an easy, humane, and obvious treatment of moral subjects by removing the "abstruse philosophy" for ever from the field—Hume tries to soften the impression of the earlier work by toning down his scepticism to a very considerable extent.

[1] Works, i. p. 236. [2] *Exam.* p. 555. [3] *Ibid.* p. 554.

He still advocates scepticism, but more by insinuation than assertion, and the scepticism is of a "mitigated" kind. In all essential respects, however, the main principles of the two words are the same. In both, "Pyrrhonism" holds the field so far as reason is concerned, though Hume in the *Enquiry* affects to jest at its "curious researches," and to temper its excess of doubt by appeal to "natural instinct."[1] But even in the *Treatise* it is not pretended that the scepticism of reason can maintain itself against the non-rational force of instinct. The very contrary:—

"It is happy," he says, in the conclusion of the passage above quoted, "therefore, that nature breaks the force of all sceptical arguments in time, and keeps them from having any considerable influence on the understanding. Were we to trust entirely to their self-destruction, that can never take place, until they have first subverted all conviction, and have totally destroyed human reason. . . . Thus the sceptic still continues to reason and believe, even though he asserts that he cannot defend his reason by reason."[2]

And later:—

"This sceptical doubt, both with respect to reason and the senses, is a malady which can never be radically cured, but must return upon us every moment, however we may chase it away, and sometimes may seem entirely free from it. It is impossible, upon any system, to defend either our understauding or our senses; and we but expose them further when we endeavour to portray them in that manner. As the sceptical doubt arises naturally from a profound and

[1] Works, iv. pp. 182–3. [2] *Ibid.* i. p. 237.

intense reflection on those subjects, it always increases the further we carry our reflections, whether in opposition or conformity to it. *Carelessness and inattention alone can afford us any remedy.*"[1]

Beyond this Hume never got at any stage. This, indeed, is one feature and main point in his scepticism—to show that what our reason constrains us to regard as false and contradictory, our natural instincts compel us to believe and act upon as true. He does not deny us the luxury of believing in an external world, in the soul, in the necessary connection of causes and effects; he only shows that we have no reasonable ground for so doing—that reason is diametrically opposed to such belief. *Practically* things remain as they are; *theoretically* they are subverted. The sceptical arguments, like those of Berkeley, "admit of no answer, and produce no conviction."[2] Only when we venture to transcend the range of common experience, and begin to think or speak of such far more important subjects as God, Immortality, Providence, Creation, Destiny, does Hume bring in his "doubt" to show us that such "sublime" topics are entirely beyond our reach—are, in fact, as exercises of mind, extravagant and ridiculous. This is indeed the great use of his philosophy—to scare us from these "abstruse" studies by revealing to us the incapacity and fallibility of the mind that proposes to deal with them.

The worst effect of a scepticism like Hume's is, that it must inevitably react to vitiate the mind that indulges in it, and to unfit that mind for earnest dealing with any subject whatever. It destroys the power of close and patient investigation for the sake

[1] Works, i. p. 273. [2] *Ibid.* iv. p. 176.

of the truth itself. All throughout the reader is sensible of this defect in the works of Hume. In his later writings, especially, we are made to feel, as compared with his earlier, a growing want of strictness in method, and the absence of a fresh interest in the subjects of which he treats. On the other hand, we mark an increased elegance of style, and a more concise and effective presentation of his separate ideas. Hume's scepticism particularly unfitted him for doing justice to men whose minds were possessed by warm and earnest convictions in regard to the unseen, and whose lives were actuated by correspondingly high motives. To enter into the ideas and experiences of such men was utterly beyond his power. His two ready categories here are *superstition* and *enthusiasm*, and to one or other of these every inexplicable phenomenon in the moral and religious history of mankind is unhesitatingly referred. Hume forgets that if "practical instincts" have validity in the lower sphere, they are no less necessary and valid in the higher. Men need convictions in regard to the ideal and unseen quite as much as in reference to the seen and temporal.

A scepticism like Hume's is, as he rightly says, incurable. Diffidence in regard to the operations of intelligence in difficult and recondite subjects is one thing; distrust of the principles on which all truth and certainty depend is another. It is useless to ask in Hume's philosophy whether the error may not lie in the road by which conclusions have been reached, and whether another line of reasoning might not correct that error, and put us in the path of truth. The very asking of that question implies the supposition of, and comparison with, a realm of truth, to which our faculties stand in relation, and within which the discovery and recognition of truth is believed to be possible. Such a conception of a rationally-constituted universe, to which reason in man stands in essential relation, is precisely what Hume's philosophy excludes. It is not considered that the very fact that man can conceive of such a region of truth, even so far as to be at the trouble of denying the power of the mind to reach it, is itself a proof of its existence; for the mind that can deny rationality in the universe, in the very act of its doing so proclaims itself rational, and the universe as well.

CHAPTER VI

Hume and the First Principles of Knowledge

THERE is abundant evidence that Hume regarded himself as an original discoverer in philosophy. He speaks repeatedly and complacently of "my system." He is confident that he has succeeded where others had failed in establishing the theory of human nature upon a just foundation. It has now to be asked whether his own contributions to the doctrine of knowledge will prove more permanent than those of his predecessors; or whether, as he wrote to Hutcheson, that "in a cool hour" he was apt to suspect most of his reasonings "will be found more useful in furnishing hints and awakening curiosity, than as containing principles that will augment the stock of knowledge that must pass to future ages." [1]

The basis of Hume's system is laid in his chapters on "The Origin of Ideas." [2] Here he connects himself with Locke, but with significant changes of nomenclature. Locke had used "ideas" as the general designation for all mental acts and states. The name Hume uses for the same purpose is "perceptions"—a designation in every way as open to criticism. Locke had no distinction of terms for an idea in its first vivid

[1] Burton, i. p. 118.

[2] Works, i. pp. 16 ff.; iv. pp. 15 ff.

appearance in the mind, and its subsequent paler reproduction in memory and imagination. Hume, with more precision, distinguishes his "perceptions" into two kinds—impressions and ideas. The original element in knowledge is the "impression," under which he includes "all our sensations, passions, and emotions." The impression is given with a "force and liveliness" in consciousness peculiar to itself. "Ideas" are the fainter copies of these impressions in memory and imagination. In memory the impressions retain a considerable portion of their original vivacity; in imagination they are less forcible and vivid, and appear in new combinations. Imagination is thus with Hume, as with Hobbes, nothing more than "a decaying sense."

The next point is to prove that we have no idea which is not copied from some previous impression. Hume adduces two arguments. First, we have only to analyse our thoughts, however complex, to find that they always resolve themselves into such simple ideas as are copied from a precedent feeling or sentiment.[1] This, however, is plainly not an argument in the proper sense at all, but merely an assertion of the point to be proved. Second, if we find a man who, through a defect in the organ, is not susceptible of any particular impression, he is always found to be as little susceptible of the corresponding idea.[2] This may be granted in regard to *sensible* ideas. But the question is, Are these our only ones? Hume is not unaware that his first argument is very much a begging of the question; he therefore adds: "Those who would assert that the position is not universally true, have only one, and that a very easy method of refuting it; by producing that

[1] Works, iv. p. 17. [2] *Ibid.* iv. p. 18.

idea which in their opinion is not derived from that source."[1] This last remark might have suggested to Hume the illegitimacy of his whole procedure. Before we are competent to sit in judgment upon the origin of our ideas, it is necessary to come to some distinct understanding as to their nature. What *are* these ideas of whose origin we speak? Are they such as can all be ascribed to one source? Granted that some of them may have their origin in the senses, are there not others whose peculiar features demand for them a nobler origin?[2] As Hume leaves the matter, the way is obviously open to vast assumptions. He has not really proved that every idea is the copy of a previous impression, but has only thrown the *onus* of proof on those who differ from him. Yet, as if he *had* satisfactorily established his main position, he immediately proceeds to erect it into a universal test. "When we entertain, therefore," he says, "any suspicion that a philosophical term is employed without any meaning or idea, as is too frequent, we need but inquire, *from what impression* is that supposed idea derived?"[3] No philosopher was ever more peremptory or *a priori*

[1] Works, iv. p. 17.

[2] The truth will prove to be that even what Hume calls impressions of sensation are not mere products of sense, but involve an element of rational judgment.

[3] Works, iv. p. 20. It will afterwards appear that Hume is not consistent in the application of his own canon. It may be (1) that the philosophical term is used, as he says, "without any meaning or idea." But it may also be (2) that there *is* an idea, or *quasi*-idea, only it is a "fiction," or is due to confusion of thought. Hume would hold the ideas of self, substance, external existence, to be of this nature. Or (3) there may be a real idea, derived from an impression, but the idea is not what we take it to be. Such is the idea of necessary connection, which has, according to him, a subjective basis in the feeling of expectation.

than Hume in the application of this rule-of-thumb method of "no impression, no idea." It is not difficult to see how readily on this principle the mind may be despoiled of most of its richest possessions.

In one important respect Hume is more consistent than Locke, and rather resembles his French contemporary Condillac. Locke had distinguished between ideas of sensation and ideas of reflection, resting his distinction on the contrast of ideas received from without, and ideas received from within. But Hume more logically perceived that *without* and *within* are assumptions we are not entitled to make at starting. "All impressions," he tells us in one place, "are internal and perishing existences, and appear as such."[1] Reflection, therefore, is no separate source of ideas.[2] Locke, indeed, evades this consequence, but only by an inconsistency. He assumes, as the receptacle of his sensations, a mind, well furnished with active faculties, each working according to its own laws on the material provided to it from without. Yet there is nothing "innate"! Leibnitz well replied, *Nisi intellectus ipse.* Later empiricism, therefore, has done well to dismiss this second source of ideas altogether, and to try to get on, as best it can, with simple sensations. But in point of fact, no empiricist, not even Hume himself, adheres consistently to this original position. Hume is forced to fall back continually on certain "original principles," which, as permanent factors in our experience, and conditions of it, constitute an original "mind" of

[1] Works, i. p. 245.

[2] If, in one or two early passages, Hume adopts the Lockean phraseology (Works, i. pp. 23, 31), it has no proper place in his system, and serves only to indicate the contrast between sense-impressions and the passions and emotions.

a meagre sort, which, however, he never distinctly accounts for. Such, for instance, are his "principles of association,"[1] and the principle of "custom," of which he afterwards makes so large a use.[2] These principles of association are, it must be allowed, something of a mystery in Hume. At times they appear as original principles of the "mind" or of "human nature"; at other times they figure as mysterious powers of "attraction" between impressions and ideas themselves. "Here is a kind of attraction," he says, "which in the mental world will be found to have as extraordinary effects as in the natural."[3] How attraction can arise between ideas which, on his hypothesis, are entirely separate and "in perpetual flux and movement,"[4] is far from obvious.

The essential assumptiveness of Hume's philosophy receives much stronger illustration if we observe the very great liberty which, while professing to start only with impressions and ideas, Hume constantly allows himself in the use of the ordinary terminology of mind. He disavows, indeed, any assumption as to the origin of impressions.[5] These "arise in the soul," he tells us, "from unknown causes."[6] But, as the words quoted show, he does not disavow in the same way, a "mind" or "soul" as the seat of these impressions. On the contrary, he continually, and in so many words, takes its existence and operations for granted; endows it with faculties; furnishes it with "original principles"; ascribes to it powers of comparison and reasoning; concedes to it ideas of "relation"; under guise of the

[1] Works, i. pp. 25 ff.; iv. pp. 22 ff. Cf. pp. 123, 148, etc.
[2] *Ibid.* iv. pp. 50 ff.
[3] *Ibid.* i. p. 28.
[4] *Ibid.* i. pp. 312–13.
[5] *Ibid.* i. p. 16.
[6] *Ibid.* i. p. 22.

personal pronouns ("I," "we," etc.), makes unceasing drafts on its activity. This peculiarity is so marked, and so much depends on it for the right understanding of Hume's philosophy, that space may profitably be spared for a few examples (the italics are ours):—

"I first *make myself certain by a new review*, of what I have already asserted, that every simple impression is attended by a corresponding idea. . . . *I immediately conclude* that there is a great connection between our correspondent impressions and ideas."[1] . . . "Of this impression *there is a copy taken by the mind* which remains after the impression ceases."[2] . . . "The *faculty* by which *we repeat* our impressions in the first manner is called the *memory*, and the other the *imagination*."[3] . . . "*The liberty of the imagination* to transpose and change its ideas."[4] . . . "Whenever the imagination *perceives a difference* among ideas."[5] . . . "Nothing would be more unaccountable than *the operation of that faculty* were it not guided by *some universal principles*, which render it, in some measure, uniform with itself in all times and places."[6] . . . "The qualities from which this association arises, and by which *the mind is, after this manner, conveyed* from one idea to another."[7] . . . "That particular circumstance in which, even apart from the arbitrary union of two ideas in the fancy, *we may think proper to compare them*."[8] . . . "When *we have found a resemblance* among several objects that often occur to us, we apply the same name to all of them, *whatever differences we may perceive* in the degrees of

[1] Works, i. pp. 18, 19.
[2] *Ibid.* i. p. 22.
[3] *Ibid.* i. p. 23.
[4] *Ibid.* i. p. 24 (cf. p. 113).
[5] *Ibid.* i. p. 25.
[6] *Ibid.* i. p. 25.
[7] *Ibid.* i. p. 26.
[8] *Ibid.* i. p. 29.

their quality and quantity."[1] . . . "One would think the whole intellectual world of ideas *was at once subjected to our view*, and that we did nothing but *pick out* such as were most proper for our purpose. There may not, however, be any present, besides those very ideas, *that are thus collected by a kind of magical faculty in the soul*."[2] . . . "We begin to distinguish the figure from the colour by *a distinction of reason*."[3] . . "Identity is merely a quality which we attribute (to perceptions) because of the union of their ideas in the imagination when *we reflect on them*."[4]

If it is replied that this employment of current ideas and phraseology on the part of Hume is merely an accommodation to popular speech till the system is sufficiently advanced to show how these ideas can be dispensed with, the answer is that it is only by the assumption of these ideas that the system is able to get under weigh at all, and that, without their help, it could not present even a momentary appearance of plausibility. Suppose, for instance, we hold Hume strictly to his impressions and ideas, and ask the question, How does he *know* that his ideas are faint "copies" of previous impressions, as he tells us they are? what answer could he give? The two, to be compared, must have been present at some point in consciousness together. But the impression *ex hypothesi* has vanished before the idea comes upon the scene. When the comparison is made, there is nothing present but the assumed copy. What then yields the knowledge of its resemblance to the impression, or what or who is to make the comparison between

[1] Works, i. p. 36. [2] *Ibid.* i. p. 41.
[3] *Ibid.* i. p. 43. [4] *Ibid.* i. p. 321.

them?[1] If it is said that memory retains the image of the past impression, this is only to repeat that a "faint" idea is present, which, for some reason unknown, we take to be a copy of a former "lively" state. And the "lively" state is now known to us only through the idea. But the same difficulty recurs in regard to memory itself. Memory differs from imagination, Hume tells us, not only in the livelier character of its ideas, but in the fact that it is "tied down" to the same "order and form" as the original impression.[2] This, it may be remarked to begin with, is in no way a complete account of memory. In memory an image is not only given, but is recognised *as the image of a past event or experience.* It is connected with an idea of past *time,* and is accompanied by *belief* in the fidelity of the representation. But, in the next place, the theory leaves us entirely in the dark as to how we become *aware* that the image in memory represents the "order and form" of a past experience. "Belief," with Hume, is simply "a lively idea related to, or associated with, a present impression."[3] But the mere liveliness of an idea is surely no guarantee that it is an accurate copy of a past (and now vanished) impression. Nor is a solution possible on Hume's principles. The real and only key to the possibility of recall in memory is that persistence of the self which Hume ignores. The self, which is one and the same throughout, knows the acts which it images to itself *as its own acts.* With this has to

[1] Note the curious assumption in Hume that it is the original impression that is making "a new appearance" in the idea. Of course, on his theory, the idea is an entirely new and separate mental fact.

[2] Works, i. p. 24.

[3] *Ibid.* i. p. 128; iv. p. 56.

be taken the fact that in no case is memory the mere reproduction of a sense impression. Even in perception, as will appear later, the "impression" has passed into the form of thought—has become fixed in permanent relations—and so is preserved in its abiding character as knowledge.

These considerations open the way for a more fundamental criticism of Hume's positions.

It has just been seen that Hume's theory has not gone far before it has involved itself in considerable difficulties, rendering necessary, not only the borrowing of a number of new principles, but a somewhat abundant use of the terminology of personal consciousness. The crucial question that now arises is—Is this construction of knowledge without a conscious thinking principle to unite and combine the various parts of that knowledge possible? Both Reid and Kant assailed the account given by Hume of the *nature* of knowledge. They took up the challenge to produce an idea which has not its prototype in a sense-impression, and showed that a quality attaches to many of our ideas and judgments for which the theory of Hume, or any theory which traces all our knowledge to sensation, can never adequately account.[1] But Kant had a deeper way of attacking the problem. He goes back from the *nature* to the more fundamental question of the *possibility* of knowledge, and lays down as self-evident the proposition that there can be no knowledge of any kind except on the supposition of a principle of synthesis in consciousness—of a relation of "impressions and ideas" (to use Hume's phrase) to a central "self." "The 'I think,'" in his

[1] See below, p. 118.

own words, "accompanies all my representations."[1] We may illustrate this by a remark of Mr. J. S. Mill's on the ultimate nature of belief in memory. "Our belief in the veracity of memory," that writer says, "is evidently ultimate; no reason can be given for it which does not presuppose the belief, and assume it to be well founded."[2] This involves an important principle. That is ultimate in knowledge for which no reason can be given which does not presuppose the thing to be explained. Now what Mr. Mill here grants to be true of memory, Kant shows to be true of all sensible experience; there are certain things involved in it which can never be explained by the experience, because the experience itself presupposes them. And most fundamental of all is this condition, that impressions can only become impressions *for me* if they exist together in a common self-consciousness. I know a thing in consciousness only as I relate it with the other elements of consciousness to *myself*. Self-consciousness, in other words, with all that it involves, is an ultimate fact, and any attempt to explain it by the chemistry of association, is a case of circle-reasoning of the most glaring kind.

It will be obvious that this principle, if admitted, is fatal to Hume's whole theory of the origin of knowledge. "A train of impressions and ideas"—but how do we know them *as a train?* "A bundle or collection of different perceptions"[3]—but what holds the bundle together, or knows it as a *bundle?* The perceptions are, on Hume's showing, "in perpetual flux and movement."[4] Each, at the most, knows itself in the single

[1] *Kritik*, p. 21 (Bohn).
[2] *Exam. of Ham.* p. 174.
[3] Works, i. p. 312.
[4] *Ibid.*

moment of its existence, and knows nothing of the others. One perception has perished before another appears; what holds the vanished members of the series in knowledge, and now represents the whole as a succession? Single impressions and ideas are one thing; the idea of a *succession* is another. Applying Hume's canon to it, we may ask, From what impression is it derived? But it has already been seen that Hume does not succeed in dispensing with this relating principle. The "we" thrusts in its head at every point in his expositions, engaged in the most essential operations. We "make a review" of facts of consciousness; we "compare" ideas; we "perceive" resemblances and difference; we "reflect" on experiences, and draw conclusions; "when we have found a resemblance" we give names. Take away the implied self from these operations, and what is left of them? On this first rock, therefore, Hume's philosophy, with every other which rests on a like empirical basis, is already irretrievably shattered.

But this first step in the criticism of Hume's theory leads immediately to a second. It has hitherto been assumed, in accordance with Hume's principles, that impressions and ideas are something wholly subjective—"internal perishing existences." On psychological grounds, however, this position also must be pronounced untenable. The "I" or self, viewed as the principle of relation among the elements of consciousness, is, after all, only an abstraction. The "I" never subsists in consciousness by itself—without relation to something else, which it distinguishes from itself as *object*. In plain terms, as thinkers of all schools are now well agreed, there is no subject-consciousness which has not as its invariable counterpart an object-consciousness. This is a fact which evidently deserves careful attention. In both the "primary" and the "secondary" qualities of Locke we found that, however illegitimately on his principles, there was involved a reference to an outward world. But this answers to the fact of consciousness itself. From the first dawn of conscious life the subject- and the object-consciousness grow up together. There is, as Kant again showed, no uniting together of the elements of personal consciousness which has not as its correlate the uniting of other elements in that consciousness in the form of an objective experience. This raises more definitely the question—What precisely is meant by an "object"? Here we come on another fundamental ambiguity in Hume's system. Hume can as little dispense with the idea of the "object" as with the idea of "self." His pages teem with references to "objects," of which we are assumed to have knowledge. But two things here require to be distinguished which Hume, in his philosophy, as constantly confounds. One is the order or succession of impressions and ideas within the mind—*the subjective succession;* the other is the order or succession of phenomena in nature—*the objective succession.* The order of succession in consciousness is, of course, in part determined by the order in nature; *e.g.*, I hear the report of a gun, and observe a bird fall. Still it is evident that the current of my thoughts is one thing, and the order of events in nature is another, and there is no necessary correspondence between them. When we speak of an objective order, as will be seen more clearly later, we mean by it something which we definitely distinguish from our own thoughts;

which has a connection, coherence, and progress of its own, determined by its own laws; which exists in at least relative independence of our knowledge of it. And the important fact to be observed is, that when we speak of "object," it is this external order of nature, not the internal succession, we have in view. For me to speak of a thing as an "object" means that I place it definitely in this system or order which I distinguish from myself; that I regard it as having its fixed place and coherence in that order; as set in determinate relations with the other parts of the order; as connected with it in what goes before and what comes after,—in short, as belonging to *it*, and not to the course of my individual thoughts. It is, as we shall come to see, by habitually confounding two orders, and illegitimately passing from one to the other in his reasonings, that Hume is able to persuade himself that he has solved the problem of causation by "custom," and can even imagine, in the end of his *Treatise*, that he explains by association how the "fiction" of the idea of an independently existing world is arrived at.

Kant's answer to Hume on this as on the other point, then, is—that an object-consciousness, or idea of an objective system, is already implied in the possession of the subject-consciousness from which Hume would derive it, and that the essential principles which go to constitute that object-consciousness must be furnished by reason itself, since they antecede experience, and are the conditions of its possibility. Thus far Kant, we take it, is irrefutable; but he laid himself open to criticism equally with Hume when he held that these principles which we employ in knowledge are only principles of our own thought, and not principles constitutive of the world itself. This, however, opens up questions which belong to a later part of our investigation.

One important result which accrues from these inquiries is, that *the object is given only in relations*, and therefore can never be, as Locke and Hume would have it, a mere *datum* of sense. There is at least the act by which I relate it to myself in consciousness; but there are also the acts by which I relate it to the other objects of the world of which it forms part—through which, in fact, I constitute it "object." This, indeed, is what is properly called "knowledge"—not the passive reception of impressions, but the apprehension of objects under their permanent relations. This leads, as a third test of Hume's theory, to a glance at his doctrine of *relations*. Kant, it is well known, analysed the relations through which our knowledge is constituted into two groups: forms of intuition, and categories of the understanding. The first condition of the knowledge of objects in an outward world is that I apprehend them under the forms of space and time; then I cognize and unite them through the understanding under such categories as unity and plurality, substance and accident, cause and effect. It will be sufficient here to keep to the list of relations which Hume himself gives. It may easily be shown that the admission of ideas of relation of any kind—and Hume admits no fewer than seven heads of them: resemblance, identity, space and time, quantity and number, degree, contrariety, cause and effect[1]—is irreconcilable with the primary assumptions of his theory.

[1] Works, i. p. 95.

In the first place, a relation implies *two* terms, and a comparison between them which gives rise to the idea, and therefore is unthinkable except on the supposition of a relating principle such as has been seen to be implied in all knowledge. And in the next place, an idea of relation is not, and for this very reason cannot be, an idea of sense. It is not the copy of a sense-impression, but is the product of an intellectual act.[1] We have just seen, besides, that relations play a much larger part in the constitution of our knowledge than Hume allowed. Every object is given in relations as the condition of its being known at all. It exists in relations, and through relations is known to be what it is. In strictness it may be said that the object is much more an object of the understanding than it ever was of sense. It will be seen after how this bears on the philosophy of perception. It may now be shown that the admission of even such a list of relations as Hume gives involves problems of origin which, on his principles, are incapable of solution.

It has been stated above that both Reid and Kant took exception to Hume's account of the origin of ideas, not only on the ground that certain of these ideas are involved in all possible knowledge, but likewise because they have a character of their own which bars us from attributing to them an origin in sense. Such is the quality of *universality* and *necessity* which attaches

[1] Professor Huxley admits the inconsequence of Hume deriving ideas of relations from sense-impressions, though he himself errs (like some other psychologists) in speaking of them as "feelings." "They are," he says, "no more capable of being described than sensations are; and, as it appears to me, they are as little susceptible of analysis into simpler elements. . . . When Hume discusses relations, he falls into a chaos of confusion and self-contradiction" (*Hume*, p. 69).

to many of our ideas and judgments, as, *e.g.*, to our ideas of space and time and number, and the mathematical sciences based on these, of cause and effect, of substance and accident. Here, then, is another crucial test for Hume's system; the account it has to give of this peculiarity in part of our knowledge. We leave out of consideration for the present the ideas of cause and substance, and confine ourselves to the fundamental ideas of space and time. This is a test-case for Hume, as for the schools descended from him, and it need not be said that he entirely fails to show the origin of these ideas from sense-impressions. It is not that he does not make the attempt. He discusses the ideas of space and time at great length, and with much ingenuity, in his *Treatise*. They are for him "no separate and distinct ideas, but merely those of the manner or order in which bodies exist."[1] "As it is from the disposition of visible and tangible objects we receive the idea of space, so from the succession of ideas and impressions we form the idea of time."[2] Precisely; but it is strange it did not occur to so acute a reasoner that to derive the idea of space from the "manner or order" in which visible and tangible objects are "disposed," or the idea of time from the "succession" of impressions and ideas, is simply, under a change of phraseology, to derive these ideas from themselves. The "distinct ideas" sought for are already implied in the expressions used. For the "manner or order" of the "disposition" of visible and tangible bodies, means simply their arrangement in a particular manner *in space;* and the "succession" of impressions and ideas means simply that they are

[1] Works, i. p. 60. [2] *Ibid.* i. p. 54.

cognized as one after another *in time*. On this latter point Reid aptly remarks in his criticism of Locke, that "it would be more proper to derive the idea of succession from that of duration," than *vice versâ*, "because succession presupposes duration, and can in no sense be prior to it."[1] Time, in other words, as Kant showed more thoroughly, is already implied in all apprehension of succession, and to derive the former from the latter is a case of the old fallacy of explaining a thing by itself. It is not otherwise with the attempts to derive the idea of space from the perception of "distance" or "extension"; as if "distance" were anything else than spatial remoteness, or "extension" (*partes extra partes*) could be defined except in terms of space. Mr. Mill says in one place: "Whatever else we may suppose removed, there always remains the conception of empty space."[2] If this is so, space is a distinct and necessary idea, and is not to be confused with the idea of the extension of material objects, which are *in* space. A favourite device of a certain school of psychologists has been to derive the idea of space from that of time. Dr. Thomas Brown did his best to explain in this way the genesis of the ideas of space and extension; and his efforts in this direction were heartily seconded by the two Mills, and later by Mr. Bain.[3] Even if the attempt had been as successful as it was really the reverse, it would still have left the idea of *time* to be explained. Kant, in truth, had already met by anticipation this attempt of the Association school to confound the ideas of space and time by deriving the one from the other. So far, he argued, are we from the deriving the idea of

[1] Hamilton's *Reid*, pp. 347–8. [2] *Exam. of Ham.* p. 291.

[3] Mill, *ibid.* pp. 227 ff.; Bain, *Mental and Moral Science*, pp. 48 ff.

space from that of time, that we can only picture the latter to our imagination through an image of the former. We figure duration to ourselves as a drawn-out line.[1]

Hume's boldness in deriving all our ideas from sense-impressions reaches its culmination in his attempts to explain in this manner even the pure ideas of "geometry, algebra, and arithmetic."[2] This, while conceding that the relations involved in these ideas are "intuitively or demonstratively certain."[3] Kant remarks that if Hume had only considered this point as carefully as he did the fact of causation, he would have been saved from many of his conclusions. He came nearest of all philosophers to a solution of the great problem, but failed, because "it never acquired in his mind sufficient precision, nor did he regard the question in its universality."[4]

[1] *Kritik*, p. 95 (Bohn).
[2] *Treatise*, bk. i. pt. ii.
[3] Works, iv. p. 30.
[4] *Kritik*, pp. 12, 13 (Bohn).

CHAPTER VII

HUME ON CAUSE AND EFFECT: FREE-WILL

HUME'S theory may be said to concentrate itself in his doctrine of cause and effect. He himself doubtless felt this to be the strongest and most original part of his system, and in the later edition of his philosophy he spared no pains in perfecting it. Viewed as a carrying out of his principles to their legitimate issues, his reasonings have all the force of demonstration. They end by depriving the notion of cause and effect of all real validity. It is merely, in Hamilton's terse description, "the offspring of experience engendered on custom." [1]

In a familiar passage, Hume divides all objects of knowledge into two classes: relations of ideas and matters of fact.[2] Relations of ideas yield us knowledge which is either intuitively or demonstrably certain; in regard to matters of fact, on the other hand, the one relation which carries us beyond the experience we have, and gives us new knowledge, is that of cause and effect. *A priori* argument avails us nothing here; our knowledge of everything that lies beyond the immediate impression of sense must be deduced, by a longer or shorter train of reasoning,

[1] *Lects. on Met.* ii. p. 394.

[2] Works, iv. pp. 30, 41.

through this single principle of causation. If, therefore, this pillar of the house of knowledge is overthrown, the whole edifice of our reasonings in regard to matters of fact is brought to the ground. To show, accordingly, that this is how the case actually stands with respect to causation—that there is, in reality, no rational basis for our belief in the connection of causes and effects, nor any necessary principle connecting the phenomena we so denominate—is the end to which Hume applies himself with all his force. He has to show, first, that the ordinary belief in cause and effect is without rational justification; and, second, what the real origin and nature of this belief is.

The first point to be established is, that the relation of causes and effects is one which is discoverable only by experience. Reason can furnish us with no aid in determining what particular effects will follow from particular causes. No man, *e.g.*, could predict, prior to experience, that fire would burn, or water drown him. This must, of course, be admitted, but it has often been pointed out that it evades the real question at issue. This is not, whether, before experience, we can tell what *particular* effects will follow from *particular* causes, but whether, either before experience or after it, we can believe that any change or event will ever happen without *some* cause. There is an obvious distinction between *a* cause and *the* cause. This Hume must admit, for he afterwards assumes that it is possible to strip the causal judgment of its original particularity, and erect it into a universal principle.[1]

[1] Works, iv. pp. 105–6, 139. This, no doubt, in Hume's case, is an inconsistency. (1) His doctrine allows no place for abstract or general ideas, so leaves no room for general principles deduced from

What we have found to be true of particular cases, we come to assume will be true of all others. But if we can thus universalise our judgments, then we are able to affirm that there must be a cause, even where we are ignorant of *what* it is.

The knowledge of causes and effects being thus traced solely to *experience*, the question which next arises is, What is there in experience which can generate this idea?

"When it is asked," says Hume, "What is the nature of all our reasonings concerning matters of fact? the proper answer seems to be, that they are founded on the relation of cause and effect. When, again, it is asked, What is the foundation of all our reasoning and conclusions concerning that relation? it may be replied in one word, *Experience*. But if we still carry on our sifting humour, and ask, What is the foundation of all our conclusions from experience? this implies a new question which may be of more difficult solution and explication."[1]

There are several difficulties to be got over. (1) Experience gives us only "loose and separate" events,[2] but the relation of cause and effect is supposed to be that of necessary connection. (2) Experience gives us information of those precise objects only which fall under our cognizance; but this does not explain why we should extend this experience to other and different objects. (3) Experience relates only to what has been

particular instances; and (2) the utmost his theory of association will yield him is, that antecedents similar to those observed might be supposed to have similar consequents, not that there is a necessary relation between antecedents and consequents generally.

[1] Works, iv. p. 38.

[2] *Ibid.* iv. p. 84.

observed in the past; but the inference from cause and effect is extended into the future. "We always presume," he says, "when we see like sensible qualities, that they have like secret powers, and expect that effects similar to those which we have experienced will follow from them. . . . Now this is a process of the mind of which I would willingly know the foundation."[1] Hume then shows that this inference from the past to the future, however it is to be explained, is not founded on any *process of argument.* These two propositions are far from being the same—"I have found that such an object has always been attended with such an effect," and, "I foresee that other objects which are in appearance similar, will be attended with similar effects."[2] If the inference is made by reasoning, there should be some middle term which connects he two judgments; but this, of course, can never be produced. He concludes, therefore, with perfect justice, that the uniformity of the operation of causes and effects which would enable us to infer the future from the past, can never be proved by argument.

It may be questioned, however, whether Hume is not here chargeable with another confusion, besides that of constantly identifying the question of a cause with that of some particular cause. He rightly assumes that when we find a cause in nature we expect it to operate uniformly. The idea of a *cause,* nevertheless, is not quite the same as that of the *uniform operation* of the cause. "I say, then," he himself remarks, "that even after we have experience of the operations of cause and effect, our conclusions from that experience are not founded on reasoning."[3] The experience of

[1] Works, iv. p. 39. [2] *Ibid.* iv. p. 40. [3] *Ibid.* iv. p. 38.

the operation of causes, then, precedes, and is distinct from, the discovery that they operate uniformly. The distinction may be perceived if we reflect on the phenomena of volition, or think of that crude stage in the history of mankind when effects in nature are ascribed to the volition of living agents. Here there is causation, but it is conceived of as capricious and irregular. The ground of our expectation of uniformity in the operation of causes will be investigated later.

The main difficulty Hume has to encounter is the apparent existence of an "idea of necessary connection" in the causal judgment. He treats of this in a separate Essay, but it is really the same question as he had previously before him. We infer that the future in natural operations will resemble the past because we have already somehow come to believe in the necessary connection of events. The gist of Hume's theory lies, therefore, in the explanation he has to give of this idea of necessary connection. He first shows that no such necessary connection is implied in anything given directly by observation. He easily refutes Locke's doctrine that we receive the idea from sensation and reflection. What we observe is simply constant succession, or constant conjunction; of a supposed bond or connection between events, the experience of the senses can teach us nothing.[1] He argues with great force that the idea cannot be derived even from the consciousness of our acts of volition. His arguments on this point are in part valid against

[1] "All events seem entirely loose and separate. One event follows another, but we can never observe any tie between them. They seem *conjoined*, but never *connected*' (Works, iv. p. 84).

Maine de Biran and others of the French school, who adopt this explanation; and against Mansel, who supposes that we transfer the idea of cause, gained from the power of the will over its own determinations, to beings and objects generally.[1] We do know ourselves as spiritual causes, but this recognition already implies the idea of causation, and the legitimacy of the transference of the idea to nature, and universalising of it, is not obvious. Failing every other explanation, therefore, Hume falls back on CUSTOM, in which he claims to find the solution of the problem. When we have had frequent experience of similar conjunctions of events, a connection between the two is firmly established in the mind. The presence of the one event naturally suggests the idea of its usual attendant, and leads us to expect it. This tie, which is purely a connection between our own ideas formed by association, we transfer to the objects, and think of it as existing between *them*.[2] So arises the idea of a necessary connection among objects.

Briefly expressed, therefore, the idea of necessary connection among events is the result of custom and association uniting their ideas firmly in the mind. The mere fact of one event following another in a single instance, or in a few instances, would not of itself beget the idea of causation; but when, of two events, one is found *constantly* following the other, an association is formed which creates a firm connection in idea, and brings it about that the appearance of the one invariably suggests the idea of the

[1] *Prol. Log.* pp. 139–40; *Met.* pp. 266–8.

[2] "Necessity is something that exists in the mind, not in objects" (Works, i. p. 212).

other.[1] In the vividness of conception with which the mind is carried from the one idea to the other, consists the nature of *belief*.[2] With delightful naïveté Hume points out how this tendency is confirmed when we find that the actual order of the world is conformable to the train of our thoughts and imaginations, and speaks of this as "a kind of pre-established harmony between the course of nature and the succession of our ideas."[3]

This searching examination of the validity of the causal idea was, as every one now acknowledges, productive of the best results in philosophy. First, like Hume's other speculations, it showed men clearly what were the legitimate consequences of certain principles; and, second, it prompted them to a reinvestigation of the whole question. For it did not require a great degree of acumen to perceive that the explanation offered by Hume was far from covering all the facts. It labours under the radical defect of seeking to account for an idea, the nature and characteristics of which have never been sufficiently examined. Hume does not begin with a careful analysis of what is involved in the notion of cause, but proceeds at once to demand the impression from which the idea is derived. He admits that there is a necessary connection to be taken into account; but, instead of first examining the nature of this necessity, and then asking, as Kant did, how such an idea of necessary connection is possible, he forecloses discussion by the assumption that, if the idea is not copied from a sensible impression, it can have no meaning or validity.

[1] Works, iv. p. 85; cf. i. p. 213. [2] *Ibid.* iv. p. 56.
[3] *Ibid.* iv. p. 62.

As a preliminary criticism on the theory, a remark may be made on the peculiar place which Hume gives to the principle of custom in connection with it. It is difficult to know how precisely Hume conceives of this principle in relation to the general principles of association; whether it is supposed to be distinct, or is regarded as only a special case of the latter. At all events, it is described by him in terms which imply that it itself operates as a true cause, or force, in the mind, determining the connection of ideas. The passage is instructive:—

"By employing that word (custom), we pretend not to have given the ultimate *reason* of such a propensity. We only point out a *principle of human nature* which is universal, acknowledged, and which is well known by its *effects*. Perhaps we can push our inquiries no further, or pretend to give the *cause* of this cause; but must rest contented with it as *the ultimate principle*, which we can assign, of all our conclusions from experience."[1]

That is to say, in order to make out that causation has no real existence, Hume is compelled to assume a principle of causation operating in the very way he proposes to get rid of. Causation is to mean strictly nothing but constant conjunction of antecedent and consequent; but in order to explain how we come to have a feeling of necessary connection between these two, he presupposes a cause which is *not* an antecedent, but an "ultimate principle" of mind, determining the connection of ideas. He disproves causation by the help of a principle of causation; shows the idea to be

[1] Works, iv. p. 51. The italics call attention to the words and phrases deserving special notice.

a fiction by means of a hypothesis which assumes its reality. Similar in effect is his continual use of language which implies the reality of "power," "force," "influence," "determination," "necessity," at the very moment when he is endeavouring to disprove that the mind has any such ideas.

To see how far Hume's theory comes short of an adequate explanation of the ordinary notion of cause and effect, we may begin by quoting two passages from his writings on the nature of this relation:—

"We suppose," he says, "that there is some *connection* between them: some *power* in the one by which it *infallibly produces the other*, and *operates* with the *greatest certainty* and *strongest necessity*."[1]

Again: "When we consider the unknown circumstance in one object by which the degree or quantity of its effect is *fixed and determined*, we call that its power."[2]

It is implied in these statements that the idea of cause and effect is, as already seen, (1) that of a *necessary* connection; (2) that of an *objective* relation; and (3) involves the idea of *power*. Subsequent speculators, who have impugned the doctrine of Hume, have assailed it mainly either on the first of these grounds, showing that the confessed necessity inherent in the relation could never be engendered by custom; or on the second, showing that custom and association could never account for the idea of a "fixed and determined" order of nature. On the other hand, the Association school have substantially adopted and defended the doctrine of Hume, Mr. Mill, *e.g.*, resolutely

[1] Works, iv. p. 85.

[2] *Ibid.* iv. p. 88 (italics in both passages ours).

upholding it in his *Examination of Hamilton,* under the name of "inseparable association" for Hume's "custom." An intermediate position was occupied by Dr. Thomas Brown, who, while adopting Hume's view so far as it denied the objective connection of events, yet differed strongly from Hume on the power of custom to generate belief in the uniformity of nature. On this latter point Brown has left many acute remarks, but his own theory is not much better than the one he criticises. "Power," he says, "is nothing more than invariableness of antecedence."[1] This, however, is a simple question of fact. Do men really mean no more than Brown asserts when they speak of power? They mean, surely, by it, not only that one event *follows* another, has always followed it, and will always do so in the future, but that one object or event exercises a *determining influence* on another—has an *efficacy in producing* change in the other. This element Brown entirely leaves out. He resolves the idea of cause into that of uniformity of nature, and, after showing that custom could never account for our belief in that uniformity, calls in an ultimate principle to explain the latter. As if that principle were not itself a cause in the rejected sense. Hume is more consistent in the description he gives of power, but likewise holds the idea to be a figment, because copied from no impression. The idea of power, however, which has its root for us in the consciousness of voluntary energy, is not to be thus summarily got rid of. Not to speak of modern systems which find the principle of existence even more in "Will" than in "Idea" (Schopenhauer, Hartmann), and of the preponderant

[1] *Cause and Effect,* p. 30.

place occupied by the ideas of "force" and "energy" in modern science, it is surely a most curious inversion of Hume's position that our latest "positive" philosophy should be found basing its whole interpretation of nature and mind on the idea of Unknowable "Power"!

The objection to Hume on the ground of the *necessity* of the causal judgment has been urged by Kant (in connection with his general theory of knowledge), by Reid, Hamilton, and many others, and is the favourite argument of those who adhere to what is called the "Intuitional" school. Custom, it is pointed out, cannot explain the quality of necessity in the causal judgment. It is a judgment we make, apparently, as soon as reflection commences, and not a single fact can be adduced to show that it increases in strength as time goes on.[1] It is also a judgment we make universally; it extends to all new events, as well as to those which have been previously observed. Now, as Hamilton remarks, "Allow the force of custom to be as great as may be, it is always limited to the customary, and the customary has nothing whatever in it of the necessary. But we have here to account, not for a strong, but for an absolutely irresistible belief."[2] The reply of the empirical school to this is, that "inseparable association" *has* the power of engendering "irresistible belief," *i.e.*, of creating a feeling equivalent to necessity. Mr. Spencer adds hereditary transmission of acquired

[1] Here again cause is not to be off-hand identified with uniformity of nature, as to which our knowledge *is* clarified and strengthened by experience. But no change is ever held to be cause*less*.

[2] *Lects. on Met.* ii. p. 393. The matter, however, it seems to us, is wrongly put, when rested on subjective necessity of belief. The necessity rather lies in the nature of the truth or principle, which shines in the light of its own rational self-evidence.

beliefs as giving them enhanced strength. The difficulties of this explanation, however, become insuperable if we take into account the very stringent limits within which, by admission of the advocates of the theory, the principle of association can operate to generate an irresistible belief. "The phenomenon," Mr. Mill says, "must be so closely united to our experience, that we never perceive the one, without at the same time, or at the immediately succeeding moment, perceiving the other."[1] Again, "No frequency of conjunction between two phenomena will create an inseparable association, if counter-associations are being created all the while."[2] But can any one affirm that these conditions have ever been complied with in the case of the sequences of nature which we relate as causes and effects?

The more carefully, in fact, this theory of Hume's as to the genesis of the causal idea is examined, the more clearly it is seen to abound in assumptions and inconsequences. The explanation of belief in causal connection is thought to be found in experience of constant conjunction of objects and events. But, in the *first* place, every constant conjunction is not a case of causation. There may be antecedence and consequence, invariable so far as our experience goes, to which we yet do not attribute causal connection. To take the familiar example, day follows night, and night follows day; but it is not held that the one is the cause of the other. Else, as Reid observes, every case of habitual association would be a case of causation. There is a German proverb, "Who says A, says B," but A is not on that account held

[1] *Exam. of Ham.* p. 266. [2] *Ibid.*

to be the cause of B. The idea of even invariable sequence, therefore, is to be distinguished from that of causation. But, in the *second* place, granting, as of course we must, that causes and effects are constantly conjoined in nature, it is certainly not the case that belief in causal connection arises from experience of this constant conjunction. In how many instances do we observe changes of which the causes are wholly unknown to us? Nature is full of *apparent* irregularities. The cases in which a sequence has been observed so often as to generate a fixed belief through custom, are few in comparison with the others. "Among so many unconnected but coexisting phenomena," says Dr. Brown, "as are perpetually taking place around us, it is impossible that in the multitude of trains of sequence the parts of one train alone should always be observed by us; and the mind, therefore, even though originally led to believe in causation or original sequence, must soon be rendered doubtful of its first belief, when, from the comparison of parts of trains, the expected sequence is found to be different."[1] Again, speaking of the numberless cases in which we observe a new phenomenon, the same ingenious writer observes: "If it be the experience of custom alone which can give us that belief of connection by which we denominate a change an effect, we are in this case not merely without a customary sequence; we have not seen a single case of it. Yet there is no one who does not believe the change to be *an* effect as completely as if he had witnessed every preceding circumstance."[2] This leads to a *third* remark, that it is not the case that long experience of conjunction is needed to pro-

[1] *Cause and Effect*, p. 122. [2] *Ibid.* p. 133.

duce the conviction of causation. It is often sufficient to produce the idea of causal connection to see one clear instance of the change. The child, *e.g.*, that burns its fingers at the candle (to use an illustration of Hume's own [1]), does not need a second trial to deter it from repeating the experiment. So in science, one crucial experiment under appropriate conditions may be decisive.

We pass to yet deeper ground when we proceed, as a next step, to the second form of objection to Hume's theory—that it can render no account of the *objective* character of the judgment of causality. The force of this will be apparent in view of what has been said in the previous chapter, of our idea of an objective order. On Hume's principles, what we have passing through the mind—or rather what constitutes the mind—is simply a succession of impressions and ideas. Any conjunction or association of these is only a union of our ideas with each other. But it was before shown that there is the broadest possible distinction between the succession of our own thoughts, and the objective succession of events in nature, and that a large part of the plausibility of Hume's doctrine depends on his continually confounding these two orders—the order of thought and the order of things—with each other. On any hypothesis, it must be admitted that men *do* make this distinction between the course of their own thoughts and the objective course of nature,—we found Hume himself making the distinction, and even speaking (popularly, no doubt) of the "pre-established harmony" between them,—and there is as little doubt that when we speak of the relation of cause and effect,

[1] Works, iv. p. 45.

it is the objective order, not the subjective, we have in view. To say that fire melts wax, that prussic acid destroys life, that a storm wrecks a ship, is more than a description of a succession of impressions and ideas in the mind. It expresses a relation of these objects among themselves, and modes of their actions upon one another, irrespective of the order in which they may chance to be presented to our thoughts. In point of fact, the effect may be observed before the cause, or the cause may never be observed at all. Flame causes heat (another of Hume's illustrations), but I may perceive the heat before I am led to observe the flame. It is not without reason, therefore, that Hume is found constantly exchanging "ideas" with "objects," and affirming of the latter what is true only of the former.

But Kant goes deeper. It is essential to Hume's theory of the derivation of the causal judgment, that, prior to the possession of the idea of causality, we should observe successions of phenomena in a fixed order. It is from observation of their regular conjunctions that the idea is supposed to be obtained. It is here that Kant strikes in with his penetrating criticism. In assuming the existence of an objective world, and of orderly succession in that world, you have, he argues, already implicitly supposed the operation of that causal principle which you imagine yourself to obtain from your experience of it. For what is meant by speaking of objects, and of a succession of objects, in the natural world? To speak of a thing as object at all, is, as shown in last chapter, to give that thing a place in an order or system which has a subsistence, coherence, and connection of parts, irrespective of the course of our ideas of it. It implies an order in which the parts are definitely related to each other, in which each has its place fixed by relation to the other parts. But such an order already involves—is constituted for our thought and experience through—this very principle of causation which we are proposing to derive from it. This does not mean that in the system of nature each antecedent is regarded as the cause of its immediate consequent. But it does mean that every term in that succession has its definite place assigned to it in the order of the whole, and this is only possible through causal relations. The idea of cause may not *per se* imply that of a fixed order; but it is indisputable that the idea of a fixed order implies that of cause. Else any given phenomenon would be an accident; it might appear equally well at any point of the series of events; it would not be integrated with the other phenomena as part of an objective system. If this be clearly understood, it is fatal to the acceptance of Hume's theory, for it shows that his derivation of the causal judgment from experience of constant conjunctions is an inversion of the actual state of the case.

This enables us to give an answer to the question formerly postponed as to the real ground of our belief in the uniformity of nature. Hume wishes to know how it comes about that, having observed causation in a particular instance, we are led to extend this belief in causation to similar and future instances. The simple answer would seem to be that, *in default of reason to the contrary*, we regard bodies which exhibit similar properties, or, as Hume would say, have like sensible qualities, as being *the same in nature;* we therefore expect them to operate in the same way. That judgment may be correct, or may prove, on experiment, to be in whole or part erroneous. Objects apparently similar may really differ in some unknown respect, or the uniformity we have discovered in their action may prove liable to modification (*e.g.*, the expansion of water at freezing-point). We thus correct mistakes, and enlarge our knowledge of the true laws and constitution of nature; but our confidence is never shaken that, so far as we *have* discovered the real nature of objects, they will continue to act according to that nature. So far from reason having nothing to do with the "inference" we make, it is precisely because we believe nature to be a rationally-constituted system that we expect constancy in it.

A few words may now be said, on the basis of these discussions, on the true origin and nature of this idea of causation. Hume seeks to subvert the causal judgment by showing that it springs (to use words employed in another connection), not from the "cogitative," but from the "sensitive" part of our nature—that is, that there is no ground for it in reason. In truth, as just said, it is reason, and reason alone, that will yield it. The fundamental postulate of reason is, that whatever exists, has some rational explanation of its existence; that whatever changes take place, there is always a reason which explains these changes. A mind to which this is not self-evident on the mere statement of it, can never have it proved to it by argument. In pure thinking, at least, it will be admitted that there is a rational sequence in ideas. In a geometrical demonstration, *e.g.*, what we have is not simply one idea following upon another, and united with that other by association. There is perceived a connection in reason between the premises and the conclusion. In the world of reality it is not different. We may not perceive the reason of a change, but we have no manner of doubt that there *is* a reason, and a sufficient one. Either, as in the case of a self-determining agent, the being has the reason of the change within himself; or, as in the case of natural (selfless) phenomena, the object is determined to be what it is by something beyond itself. It is this idea of established connection on some rational principle which we denominate "necessary connection" in nature—a connection not indeed *metaphysically* necessary, as if the constitution of nature might not conceivably have been other than it is, but *factually* necessary. Metaphysical necessity inheres only in the rational principle that a cause or reason there must be. When, accordingly, Hume says that there is never perceived any rational connection between cause and effect, he greatly oversteps the evidence. A man frames, we shall suppose, the plan of a house or design of a machine; will any one say that when his plan or design is executed, it is simply a case of one thing following another, and that there is no rational connecting principle between means and end? When a writer like Hume conceives a book intended to convey to other minds an idea of a particular philosophical system, will any one affirm that there is no connection save that of accidental succession between the thoughts of the original author, the book he has produced, and the impression it makes upon the reader? Even in external nature, if the laws concerned in the production of a particular phenomenon are clearly grasped,—say the laws of chemical combination,—is it correct to say that you cannot, up to a certain point, give a rational explanation of the effects that are produced? Else what do we mean by explanation? The result of the whole is, that Hume's endeavour to get rid of reason in the sphere of causation is as vain as his efforts to explain the rise of knowledge without a conscious, thinking mind, without rational principles of connection among ideas, and without the recognition of an objective world, by reference to which our internal states are known to *be* internal.

In closing this chapter, allusion must be made to one other topic directly connected with the subject of causation. None of the great speculators on causation have left out of view the bearings of their doctrine on Free-Will; and Hume likewise has an application of his theory to "Liberty and Necessity," in which he consistently reduces all human action to the same law of necessity as prevails in nature. "Thus it appears," he says, "that the conjunction between motives and voluntary actions is as regular as that between cause and effect in any part of nature;[1] while he defines liberty as simply "a power of acting or not acting according to the determinations of the will."[2] And at first Hume seems justified; for if causation is a necessary principle of connection among phenomena, how shall volitions, any more than other phenomena, be withdrawn from its scope?

One answer that might be given, which is also in part Kant's, is that causation applies only to nature—to the phenomenal world—not to the world of spirit. In the outward world necessity rules; in mind or spirit, freedom. Dugald Stewart wrote: "This maxim (that

[1] Works, iv. p. 100. [2] *Ibid.* p. 107.

every change implies the operation of a cause), although true with respect to inanimate matter, does not apply to intelligent agents, which cannot be conceived without the power of self-determination." The obvious fault of this statement is, that it does not cover all the facts. It is not true that causation is confined only to the objective world, or to inanimate nature. The will itself is a cause, and acts outwards on nature, as well as in the regulation of thought and conduct. The principle of causation does not apply only to changes in nature, but to the fact of *change as such*. In a large part (the involuntary part) of our inward life—in the sensitive nature, the passions, the emotions, the workings of association and habit—the reign of causation is as obvious as in the world of matter.

Yet probably it is in this line of what Kant says of causation as a category of nature that the real solution of our problem is to be sought. If, as was previously urged, it is the "I" which is the relating principle in knowledge—that which relates objects in their causal, as in other, connections—it seems obvious that it cannot itself be treated as one of the objects which it helps to relate. It is above the natural order, with its laws of causation. This is viewing the self as *thinking*, but the same applies to it as acting—as *will*. In the simple fact of self-consciousness, the self knows itself raised above nature with its law of external necessitation—of determination *ab extra*. To it belongs the power, which is wanting to external nature, of distinguishing itself from objects without, and from desires and passions within, and of determining itself freely in light of principles and ends. Man, as Kant says, is a being that acts under the representation of ends. This does not mean that the will at any time acts without reason or motive; for every act of a free, rational nature, there will always be a "why." But it is given to the self to determine itself *ab intra;* it is a cause which originates action, but is not itself an effect. Through unfaithfulness or vicious choice, a man may, indeed, part with this high prerogative, and become the slave of passion: it is the problem of our moral condition that we do find ourselves in alienation from our truest selves, and in bondage to evil. But regarded in the light of his essential nature, man's dignity consists in his power of self-determination, and in regulation of his life by rational and moral ends.

In human freedom, therefore, there is no contradiction of the law of causation, but rather the raising of that law to its own ultimate principle in self-conscious personality. It is but following out the same thought, if we come to see that the final explanation of the causal order even of nature—of the objective system—must lie, not in an infinite regress of finite causes and effects, but in a principle on which the whole depends; a principle rational and self-conscious—in Spinoza's phrase, but in a personal sense, *Causa sui.*

CHAPTER VIII

HUME ON SUBSTANCE—THE MATERIAL WORLD: THE EGO

THE two great metaphysical categories are those of *causality* and *substance.* On them rests the entire structure of physical science. The natural philosopher must assume the unconditional validity of the principle of causation; not less implicitly must he assume the principle of the indestructibility of substance. All his reasonings and calculations would else be abortive. The sceptic, therefore, who can subvert these two important categories by showing them to be chimerical and unreal, may justly claim to have overturned the whole fabric of knowledge. It has been shown how Hume attempted to achieve this with regard to the category of cause. It is now to be considered how it fares with his assault on the second of these categories —that of substance.

Substance we found to be one of the ideas which caused Locke particular difficulty. He was unwilling to part with it; he upheld to the last its validity; but he could give no intelligible account of it. The senses reveal to us only qualities of objects— colours, sounds, tastes, hardness, etc.; they tell us nothing of an unknown something in which these qualities inhere. Hume was less considerate and more consistent.

"I would fain ask those philosophers," he says, "who found so much of their reasonings on the distinction of substance and accident, and imagine we have clear ideas of each, whether the idea of substance be derived from the impressions of sensation and reflection? If it be conveyed to us by our senses, I ask, which of them, and after what manner? If it be perceived by the eyes, it must be a colour; if by the ears, a sound; if by the palate, a taste; and so of the other senses. But I believe that none will assert that substance is either a colour, or sound, or a taste. The idea of substance must therefore be derived from the impression of reflection, if it really exist. But the impressions of reflection resolve themselves into our passions and emotions, none of which can possibly represent a substance. We have, therefore, no idea of substance distinct from that of a collection of particular qualities, nor have we any other meaning when we either talk or reason concerning it.

"The idea of a substance as well as that of a mode, is nothing but a collection of simple ideas, that are united by the imagination, and have a particular name assigned them, by which we are able to recall, either to ourselves or others, that collection." [1]

The language of Dr. Thomas Brown is almost identical with that of Hume on this subject.[2] So too is that of J. S. Mill in his *Logic*,[3] though in his *Examination of Hamilton* he is forced to add something to his view by the introduction of "permanent possibilities of

[1] Works, i. pp. 31, 32.

[2] *Cause and Effect*, Note C, p. 499.

[3] *Logic*, i. p. 63.

sensation." In Mr. Spencer, substance expresses the persistence of the Unknowable Power (Force), which is the ultimate reality behind both matter and mind.[1]

This denial of the idea of substance by Hume leads naturally to certain important sceptical results.

1. And, first, as the consequence of this denial, there falls necessarily the idea of an independently existing material world. Here, also, we saw that Locke was guilty of several patent inconsistencies. Assuming, to account for his ideas, a world of objects outside the mind, he began by taking this external world for granted, and only when his theory was completed, considered the question of his *right* to make so vast an assumption. Hume proceeds more regularly, and examines at length the question of the veracity of the senses in Pt. iv. sec. 2 of his *Treatise*. He assumes as a point which admits of no doubt, that men do believe in the existence of body, that is, in its continued and distinct existence, and proposes to investigate the causes wherefore they do so. The opinion must arise either from the senses, the reason, or the imagination. But it cannot arise from the senses, for these give only isolated perceptions, and say nothing of existences which lie beyond. As little can this opinion arise from reason, for reason teaches, *first*, that nothing can ever be present to the mind but its own perceptions; and, *second*, that perceptions can only exist while they are actually perceived. So far we have little more than a reproduction of the Berkeleian idealism. To reconcile these contradictions, philosophers (*e.g.*, Locke) have feigned a world of objects which lie beyond ideas and produce them.

[1] *Principles of Psychology*, i. pt. ii. ch. i.

But this is not only in itself absurd and opposed to popular belief, but it is incapable of proof. The vulgar idea of the natural world is simply that of the continued existence of the sense-perceptions themselves.[1] The belief must therefore be due to imagination. Hume accordingly attempts to show how it can be accounted for by the principles of association, co-operating with the *coherence* and *constancy* of the sense appearances, and with a "propensity to feign" continued existence in the case of interrupted perceptions.[2] The result is that we are compelled by irresistible instinct to believe in the independent existence of material things, while, on the other hand, the slightest reflection demonstrates this belief to be an illusion.

"The opinion of external existence, if rested on natural instinct, is contrary to reason, and, if referred to reason, is contrary to natural instinct, and carries no rational evidence with it to convince an impartial inquirer."[3]

[1] It is certain, on the other hand, that mankind generally distinguish the objects they perceive from their perceptions, and regard them as *other* than their perceptions. Even as regards the so-called "secondary qualities," the "vulgar" are quite capable of discerning that the *sweet taste* they feel is in them and not in the sugar, the *burning sensation* in them, and not in the poker that touches them, etc. They can distinguish the objects from their sensations.

[2] Works, i. p. 262.

[3] *Ibid.* iv. p. 177. Wundt may be compared. The external world is explained through "ideas which we distinguish as objects and images of objects." The idea of an external world is "that of a sum-total of objects"; and it is granted that "external nature is a constituent part of our consciousness." *But*, "it belongs to our inner experience just as much as any single object does, and has no reality apart from the experiences" (*Ethics*, ii. p. 44, Eng. tr.). So, "matter is a hypothetical conception which we ourselves, impelled on the one hand by the

It is very remarkable that when Hume is dwelling on the fact that "all these objects (mountains, houses, trees, etc.) to which we attribute a continued existence have a peculiar *constancy*, which distinguishes them from the impressions whose existence depends on our perceptions," and that even in their changes "they preserve a *coherence*, and have a regular dependence on each other"[1] (the fire, *e.g.*, we left burning is extinct by the time we return), he does not perceive that he is already assuming the existence of that very objective order for which it is his business to account. It is not as "fleeting and perishing" internal impressions[2] that our perceptions exhibit this constancy and coherence, but as presenting objects to the mind under independent relations of coexistence, succession, and causation.

2. But, second, rejecting the notion of an external world, have we any better ground for asserting the reality, permanence, and distinct existence of the *mind* or *self*? The discussion of this subject is omitted in the later *Enquiry*, but the question is fully gone into in the *Treatise*, sec. 6, "of Personal Identity," and elsewhere. In these places Hume clearly shows that on his original principles we must dismiss the idea of a *self*, as well as that of material objects.

"What we call a mind," he says, "is nothing but a heap or collection of different perceptions, united together by certain relations, and supposed, though falsely, to be endowed with perfect simplicity and identity."[3]

relative constancy of objects, and on the other by the logical demands of thought, have manufactured" (p. 46).

[1] Works, i. p. 246. [2] *Ibid.* i. pp. 246–7. [3] *Ibid.* i. p. 260.

More expressly: "Setting aside some metaphysicians of this kind, I may venture to affirm of the rest of mankind, that they are nothing but a bundle or collection of different perceptions, which succeed each other with an inconceivable rapidity, and are in a perpetual flux and movement. . . . The mind is a kind of theatre, where several perceptions successively make their appearance; pass, repass, glide away, and mingle in an infinite variety of postures and situations. There is properly no *simplicity* in it at one time, nor *identity* in different, whatever natural propension we may have to imagine that simplicity and identity. The comparison of the theatre must not mislead us. They are the successive perceptions only that constitute the mind; nor have we the most distant notion of the place where these scenes are represented, or of the materials of which it is composed."[1]

In this uncompromising theory Hume passes far beyond Berkeley, though there are indications that the latter had also the extreme position before his mind.

It was these daringly sceptical conclusions which, as we formerly saw, awakened Reid, and prompted him to a reinvestigation of the principles from which they followed. Reid, standing on the ground of com-

[1] Works, i. pp. 312–13. Wundt, again, whom Professor James largely follows, may be compared. "The self-contradictory conception of an immaterial matter [!], a substance lacking in permanence, an infinitely divisible atom, can be regarded only as a metaphysical superfluity, which perplexes rather than facilitates our understanding of psychical life." . . . "Representations will then not be objects but processes, phenomena belonging to a ceaseless inner stream of events. Feeling, desires, and volitions will be parts of this stream, inseparable in actuality from representations, and like these the expressions of no independent existences or forces; rather possessing reality only as individual feelings, desires, or volitions" (*Ethics*, iii. pp. 46–7).

mon sense, naturally and justly regarded the attempt to disprove the permanent reality of a *self* in consciousness as the *reductio ad absurdum* of all philosophy. His reply, however, was not as profound as it might have been. He could only fall back on the resistless conviction possessed by every man, that the thoughts of which he is conscious belong to one and the same thinking principle — what he calls *himself*, — a conviction which Hume did not deny. The true answer would have been to show, as a previous chapter indicated,[1] that without the presupposition of this permanent *self* or *ego* in consciousness there could be no consciousness at all. This was the irrefutable principle enunciated by Kant in his "Deduction of the Categories," and in light of it, the untenable character of Hume's position is very apparent. Hume, in the above passage, makes *self* "nothing but a heap (or bundle) or collection of different perceptions, united together by certain relations." But what unites the perceptions in one consciousness? It cannot be the perceptions themselves, for these are "fleeting and perishing," and each has knowledge only of its own existence. What then is it which binds the perceptions into their several "bundles," or who or what perceives the relations between them? How, *e.g.*, is perception *a* known to belong to bundle A rather than to bundles B or C? How can the individual even *appear* to himself as a unity? There is no answer to these questions on the principles of Hume; none, perhaps, even on the principles of Mr. Spencer, whose "aggregates" of states of consciousness bear a doubtful resemblance to Hume's "bundles." We have only to go back to Hume's own

[1] See above, p. 112.

sentences to see how inevitably the "we" slips in, if only in "the natural propension we have to imagine" simplicity and identity. Mr. Mill indeed felt the force of some of these difficulties; but his "series of feelings aware of itself as past and future"[1] only made the position more hopeless than ever. As he himself put it, "we are reduced to the alternative of believing that the mind or ego is something different from any series of feelings or possibility of them, or of accepting the paradox that something which *ex hypothesi* is but a series of feelings, can be aware of itself as a series."[2]

It does not destroy the value of this deduction of the reality of the ego in consciousness, that, under the influence of his peculiar idealism, Kant refused to identify this "I" with the "noumenal" self, or to permit the application to it of the categories.[3] The great point against Hume is to show that there is an "I" at all in consciousness, as distinct from the particular impressions or ideas. It may be a fair question whether "substance" (which with Kant is a category of nature) is the best term to apply to a spiritual subject like the self. There need be no controversy on a question of mere nomenclature. The essential thing is the admission of a thinking principle which abides one and the same through the changing states

[1] *Exam. of Ham.* pp. 212–13.

[2] *Ibid.* p. 213. Lotze puts the point thus: "Our belief in the soul's unity rests not on our appearing to ourselves such a unity, but on our being able to appear to ourselves at all. . . . What a being appears to itself to be is not the important point; if it can appear anyhow to itself, or other things to it, it must be capable of unifying manifold phenomena in an absolute indivisibility of its nature" (*Microcosmus*, i. p. 157).

[3] Kant admits that if the phenomenal self does not represent the real self, it at least indicates its existence.

of consciousness, knows them as its own states, relates them to itself, to one another, and to objects. Hume said, "I never can catch myself at any time without a perception";[1] to which Professor Calderwood very appositely retorted that it was enough if he could catch *himself* with one. This is the self of which each one of us is conscious, and which we cannot think without assuming. The consciousness of personal identity may arise through memory, in comparison of the present state of self with a past state; but it is not through memory, as is sometimes assumed, that personal identity is *constituted*.[2] The reverse is the truth, for it is only as I am one and the same person throughout, that I retain the memory of past acts, and am able to recognise them as imaged in consciousness as my very own.

Reverting to the question of the reality of an external world—which in its connection with the theory of perception has always been the *crux* of philosophy —it is probably again to Kant that we must look for the deepest vindication, not certainly of the independent existence of the world, but of the rational character and necessity of the principle of substance implied in our apprehension of it. It has been shown in the previous discussion that the question of self and that of the reality of an objective world are far from unrelated; that they are, in fact, but different sides of the same question. There is no consciousness of self which does not include, as its inseparable correlative, the consciousness of an *other* than self, which the mind grows to apprehend as a world of "objects," with which it stands in closest relations, alike as receiving impressions from it, and as itself acting

[1] Works, i. p. 312.

[2] Cf. Butler on "Personal Identity."

upon it and effecting changes in it. This, in fact, Hume admits under the name of "vulgar belief"; but it is to be observed that, apart from vulgar belief, and speaking purely as philosopher, he is compelled continually to make the same acknowledgment. His pages, as has been shown, are full of language which has no meaning except on the assumption that there is a world of "objects," a "succession of events," a "course of nature," different and distinguishable from the subjective course of thought and feeling.[1] It is for the constitution of such a world that Kant is able to show the indispensableness and *a priori* character of the principle of substance. In the view of Hume, substance is a "fictitious" idea—the imaginary support of qualities, perceptions, states of consciousness, which are given in "heaps" or "bundles," as others would say, "groups"—without any such suggestion of invisible support. But the question is—*Are* the objects we perceive cognized as mere "bundles of perceptions," or, in Mr. Spencer's phrase, "vivid states of consciousness"? Is it not of the very idea of an object-world that it is conceived of as having a subsistence, connection, modes of action, and successions of its own—that it goes its own way, in obedience to its own laws—not necessarily in independence of

[1] Numberless passages might be quoted in illustration, but the following may suffice :—

"We may discover that though those internal impressions which we regard as fleeting and perishing [the same description is applied on previous page (p. 246) *to all* impressions] have also a certain coherence or regularity in their appearances, yet it is of a somewhat different nature from that which we discover in bodies. . . . The case is not the same with external objects. Those require a continued existence, or otherwise lose, in a great measure, the regularity of their operation (Works, i. p. 247).

all thought, but independently at least of *my* individual knowledge and experience of it? The question is not, how a "bundle of perceptions" is held together in the mind, but how a world of the kind now described can *exist?* Kant fixes on the true idea of substance as that of a permanent subsisting in the midst of change, and proves, we think irrefutably, that this idea is involved in the very possibility of such experience as we have. He does not, like Hume, raise the question as to whether we have a knowledge of an objective order; but, starting from the *fact* of such an order as given in experience, he asks only what principles of rational connection are implied in it, and finds the principle of substance to be one of them.

This important position of Kant deserves further elucidation. Others besides him have seen the need of explaining the permanent in experience; but the theories they frame to account for it would be less plausible if they paid more attention to the fact of *change*, which Kant emphasises. Mr. Mill, *e.g.*, supposes that, having found by long experience a group of attributes regularly appearing under certain circumstances, we learn to *expect* their return, and come to regard them, even when absent, as "permanent possibilities of sensation."[1] But this is by no means the prominent idea in the thought of substance. We understand by substance something which persists, not merely when *circumstances and groups of sensations remain the same*, but when all these are changing. How is the idea of substance in *this* sense to be accounted for? Association can hardly come into play here, for all appearances are against the

[1] *Exam. of Ham.* pp. 192–200, etc.

permanence. But the strongest objection to this whole group of theories turns on the point already mentioned, that one and all they fail to give an account of permanence in an *objective* system. Association may create a subjective union among ideas which have always been found together; but unquestionably it is a very different kind of bond among phenomena we are in search of when we speak of the permanence of substance. Mr. Mill himself says: "The matter composing the universe, whatever philosophical theory we hold concerning it [?], we know by experience [?] *to be constant in quantity, never beginning, never ending, only changing its form.*"[1] The truth is, that the principle of the permanence of substance which lies at the basis of our conception of an "object" cannot be manufactured by any process which does not already imply its existence. It is the firm basis of all objective experience, and to subvert it would be to destroy at once the possibility of experience and the possibility of science.

To these considerations in support of the substantiality of the material universe, the reply may be pertinently made, that we have not yet, in answer to Hume, shown how real knowledge of such a world is possible, or met his arguments in proof that what we call perception of objects is simply a subjective state. Is the proof not overwhelming, it may be said, that what we name sense-impressions are simply internal affections of mind, and not the apprehension of any qualities existing in objects without? And have we not daily corroboration of this in the fallacy of the reports which the senses bring (*e.g.*, the bent stick

[1] *Exam. of Ham.* p. 295.

in water)? On this much exploited subject of the "fallacy" of the senses, it may be sufficient to observe at present that we can only properly speak of "fallacy" by an implied contrast with a *real* order of nature, which, therefore, is assumed to exist, and to be at least in part known. Just as the physiological method of speaking of sensations as affections of (or images in) the "brain" implies the existence as *prius* of that important organ. Every one is familiar to some extent with the limits to be set to the trustworthiness of the senses; but every one is also aware that, assuming our knowledge of the objective world to be as well founded as we ordinarily suppose it to be, it is possible from the laws of light, sound, etc., to give an explanation of these alleged deceptions of the senses, which clearly enough shows how the appearances arise from which our wrong inferences are drawn. It is because there *is* an objective system, with its fixed laws, that these appearances are what they are. Still the question is not answered as to how we have this knowledge of reality external to ourselves at all. Hume's dilemma is twofold: (1) Either the object is something truly external to the mind, in which case the mind cannot know it, or even obtain a clue to the fact of its existence, since mind cannot in the nature of things overleap its own consciousness—get outside its own ideas; or (2) the object is an idea of the mind—or "bundle of perceptions" (which is his own hypothesis)—in which case there is no external world to know, and our knowledge of it is illusion.

It may be of use here to glance briefly first at some of the results brought out by Hume's speculations in the school most opposed to him—that of Reid and

Hamilton. Reid, as is well known, attacked Hume in his fundamental position that nothing can ever be present to the mind but its own perceptions—a point too readily conceded by Kant. This at least is Hamilton's interpretation of Reid; and though Reid was not always guarded in his language, yet, taking his whole position into account, it seems probable that it is the correct one. Reid meant, in other words, to defend the doctrine of what Hamilton afterwards called "Natural Realism." He did so, as usual, on the ground of common sense, or natural irresistible conviction. So far, it is a fair reply that Hume never denied the existence of that natural conviction to which Reid appealed; what he *did* attempt to show was that it was irreconcilable with reason. But beyond this, Reid met Hume on his own ground, and sought with more or less success to prove that this natural belief is not *merely* instinctive,—a product of the sensitive, and not of the cogitative part of our nature,—but is based on knowledge; *i.e., a priori* intellectual principles are involved in it. Dr. Thomas Brown, who came after, yielded the whole ground to the sceptic. He grants that the mind is conscious only of its own states, concedes that on the principles of reason the sceptical arguments admit of no reply, and has nothing to oppose to Hume but the invincible persuasion of external reality which Hume had not thought of disputing. The doctrine of Reid was taken up and developed by Sir William Hamilton. But in developing it Hamilton found so much to alter and correct, that in the end the homely Reid would have felt it hard to discover any trace of himself in his critic's recondite speculations. Hamilton's position may be described as an attempt to combine a realistic system, founded on Reid's, with a doctrine of relativity, akin in some respects to Kant's. Some of the difficulties that pressed on Reid's theory he endeavours to avoid by his distinction of Presentative and Representative Perception, and of an Organic and Extra-Organic sphere of sense-perception. In the perception of a table, *e.g.*, it is not the outward object I directly perceive, but its illuminated retinal image; in pressing the table with my hand, on the contrary, I am directly conscious of the presence of an extended, solid object, external to myself. Sense, in both cases, contributes its part, and qualifies and modifies the total impression—hence the "relativity" of all our perceptions. The counter developments in the Association school, which stand in direct lineage to Hume, need not detain us. The service of this school is the minute attention it has bestowed on the influence of association in all mental processes; but the result arrived at is the same as in Hume, viz., that belief in an external world is a product of association working on sensations which are found to have a certain coherence and constancy in their appearances. Mr. Spencer attempts a "synthesis" of the opposing views. On the metaphysical side his theory claims to be one of Realism—a "Transfigured Realism"—but on the psychological side is not unlike Hume's in seeking to show how from the association of vivid and faint states of consciousness, we come to form ideas of objects without us.[1] The modern school has

[1] Cf. Green's searching criticism in published *Works*, vol. i. The apparently intuitional character of some of our ideas, as of space and time, Mr. Spencer explains by inheritance. But inheritance cannot account for these ideas unless they lay also in the original experiences.

devoted itself specially to the investigation of the physiological conditions of perception. The value of these labours in their own sphere is very great; but their importance for the solution of the ultimate problem may easily be exaggerated.

Looking at the problem from our own standpoint, it may first be conceded that Hume is not altogether wrong in the account he gives of perception, though, at every stage, through neglect of the rational element in knowledge, his treatment is marked by oversights. He is right, *e.g.*, in his original concession of the irresistible compulsion laid on mankind—even on philosophers—to believe in the reality and continued existence of an external world, and in his vivid descriptions of the coherence and constancy of those perceptions which determine the mind to belief in that continued existence. He is right, further, in his contention that this belief is not the result of reason in the sense of *conscious ratiocination*. It is the case, as he declares, that our belief in an external world is not the product of conscious or voluntary reflection. Nature takes in hand with the formation of the judgments involved in this belief long before reflective thought awakens; and so thoroughly does she do her work, that, in the first dawn of self-conscious life, we already find ourselves in possession of the knowledge of a world which experience, while correcting many primitive judgments by more mature ones, finds in the main to be reliable. This, however, does not imply, as Hume supposes, that the process is irrational, or originates in the "sensitive" as distinguished from the "cogitative" part of our nature. It only shows that there is an unconscious operation of reason before there is a conscious one. We are here in the region of what Professor James would term "the subliminal self." We may not be able to re-think the process, but we are assured that, if we *could* re-think it, it would explain and justify the belief we have in an external world, as well as elucidate the anomalies of what we call the "illusions" of the senses.

Yet again, we found that Hume connects the immediate presentation of the object in perception with the peculiar "liveliness" of our impressions (cf. Mr. Spencer's "vivid states"); nor is he altogether wrong in this, though he states the fact inaccurately. The sensation which is always connected with perception *is* of a peculiarly lively nature, *has* an indefinable quality of vividness, which, as Hume says, distinguishes it from its image in memory and imagination. But he errs, *first*, in supposing that the perception consists merely—or in its distinctive character of perception consists at all—in this presence of sensation. In reality, as deeper analysis shows, it involves a multitude of judgments through which we define an object to ourselves as existing in relations.[1] Into it there enters likewise a large number of other elements derived from previous experience—from memory, association, acquired judgments, etc.—constituting it in its totality a highly complex fact.[2] But, *second*, Hume inverts the real relation in basing our belief in the object on the vividness of the mental impressions, whereas in truth it is our belief in the reality and presence of the object, or

[1] See above, p. 117.

[2] Cf. Green, *Works*, i. pp. 403–4; James, *Text-Book of Psychology*, pp. 163–6. "Every object appears with a fringe of relations." See also below, p. 162.

rather our immediate apprehension of it, which imparts its forcible character to our perceptions. He errs, *third*, in attributing the vividness in question to the sensè-affection alone, and in not perceiving that, from the same cause, a like character of vividness, force, and indefinable assurance, belongs to all the mental acts involved.

Two points are involved in the criticism of Hume's theory: (1) the possibility of even forming the *idea* of an external world; and (2) the possibility of the *knowledge* of that world as existing. But these two are intimately connected; for it is evident that if we can form the idea of an object distinguishable from self, there is no inherent impossibility in the existence of such an object, or in its becoming known by us as existing. Logically, on his principles, Hume ought to say, not that the idea of an external world is "fictitious," a product of imagination, but that we have no such idea at all. This, however, would be going too far. It is plainly absurd to say that the mind cannot form the idea of an object which it distinguishes from itself, and conceives of as part of an external world, when, apart from our constant consciousness of possessing such an idea, if the idea did not exist, we could not even be found disputing as to the possibility of knowing such external objects.[1]

We come, then, to the second and main point, viz., the possibility of knowing such objects if they exist. And here we venture to think that the fallacy which runs through Hume's arguments may be summed up

[1] The form of externality is space. In strictness, therefore, as has often been pointed out, it is not the world that is external to the mind, but the objects of the world (which include our bodies) that are external to one another.

in one simple proposition—that *to say we have an idea of an object is the same thing as to say that the object is an idea.* Is this proposition true? To Hume's mind it is incontestable. In his language, "ideas," "objects," "ideas of objects," all stand for the same thing—subjective states or combinations of them.[1] But is it the case? The matter may be brought to a very simple test. We leave out of account for the moment the ideas we form of the external world, and would take only the ideas we form of our fellow human-beings—of other *persons.* Does Hume, or the veriest sceptic that ever lived, mean by his denial to the mind of a power of knowing anything beyond its own ideas, to affirm that the belief he entertains in the existence of other *minds* than his own is also a chimera—a subjective illusion, or "fiction"? In consistency he ought to do this, for it is certain that we know our fellow-men in no other way than we know the external world, through our ideas of them. But it is very curious to observe that Hume in practice never reasons against the existence of other minds as he does against the existence of an external world. To do this would be to reduce his system to too palpable an absurdity. The picture of the philosopher (not the "vulgar" man) sitting down to compose a treatise directed to other minds, to convince them of the truth of speculations which implied that no minds but the philosopher's own (if even that) existed, would be too much for most people's sense of the ridiculous. Hume, therefore, makes no scruple throughout his work in assuming

[1] Sometimes the usage is ludicrous enough. *E.g.*, "The idea of Rome I place in a certain situation on the idea of an object which I call the globe" (Works, i. p. 140).

that there are other minds besides his own, to which he can, in all seriousness, address himself. But if the philosopher can do this without thereby reducing the minds of his readers to ideas,—with the calmest assurance, in fact, that they are something more,—what becomes of the principle that to have the idea of an object means that the object itself is an idea; or of the assertion that because the mind knows only its own perceptions, it can have no knowledge of beings or objects outside itself?[1] Why, if the mind is capable of knowing real existences beyond itself in the case of other *persons*, should the same power not be conceded to it in regard to external *nature?* Is my conviction of the existence of my fellow-men one whit stronger or more reasonable than my conviction of the existence of the dog running at my side, of the fowls I see strutting in the barn-yard, of the birds I hear singing in the trees?

There remains, on the assumption of the perception of an actual world, the question of the *rationale* of the act of perception, a subject which involves too many complex psychological elements to be considered in any detail here. To the *how* of the act of perception it may be impossible for us wholly to give an answer; but we are not precluded by this from a knowledge of the *that*—the fact. And in the investigation of that fact, notwithstanding all our investigations of physiological antecedents and conditions, we do not seem to get much beyond what direct consciousness yields us, viz.,—an immediate awareness, in some relation, or what comes to the same thing, under some quality, of an object, which we apprehend as existing,

[1] Mr. Mill, of course, is in the same dilemma.

and distinguish from ourselves as part of a world, with whose other parts it stands in connection. It may be a question whether, from the sense of sight alone, presenting to us, as Hume would say, coloured points disposed in a certain manner, we could attain to that consciousness of an external, solid, and extended world, to which in fact we do attain through the combination of sight with the sense of touch and experience of muscular resistance. It is *not* a question that, when the act of perception is fully analysed, it is found, as already said, to involve many elements and factors, some of them primitive, many acquired, others results of association, perhaps of inheritance, most of them probably interpretations of the sense-accompaniments of perception (muscular feelings, *e.g.*, as the indices of space relations in judging of distances, etc.)—all of which mental science cannot too narrowly investigate. But the broad fact remains, that through all we reach the apprehension of a world of objects, which increasing experience, and scientific investigation of its laws, warrant us in regarding as actually, permanently, and independently (of *our* minds) existing.

When all is said, it must be granted that an ultimate inexplicability attaches to this act in which, under sense conditions, a world which is not ourselves enters as a real factor into our knowledge. How is this possible? Only, it may be replied, on the hypothesis that the distinction between ourselves who know and the world we know is not after all final—that there is a deeper ground and ultimate unity, that the universe, including ourselves, is a single system the parts of which stand in reciprocal relation through the spiritual principle on which in the last resort the whole depends.[1] Here, however, we enter a transcendental region which leaves Hume far behind, and into which, in this connection, we need not travel further.

The conclusions we have reached may be summed up in three propositions, which, we take it, represent positions that can never finally be extruded from philosophy.

1. The first, which is the truth of *idealism*, is that the universe, however construed, can never be divorced from *intelligence* or *thought*. It is an intelligible system; is constituted through intelligence; exists for intelligence. Its ultimate principle can only be an understanding akin in nature to our own.

2. The second, which is the truth of *realism*, is that the universe, whatever it may be, is something *actual* and *independent* of man's individual consciousness. It is as much another's as mine, and as real for him as for me. It appears in our consciousness, but it is more than our consciousness. Its reality is not our knowledge of it, whatever may be its relations to knowledge absolutely. This is the point in which the school of Reid is impregnable, and in maintaining which it did its peculiar service.

3. The third, which is the truth of *relativity*, is that the universe we know is yet known to us under the *conditions* and *limitations* that belong to human consciousness,[2] and arrayed in the sense-clothing that

[1] The idea may be studied in Lotze.

[2] Even in regard to such a quality as extension, *e.g.*, we have only to reflect that there is no such thing as absolute magnitude, that with different optical organs things would appear quite differently (under different conditions the atom might be a world, or the microbe a monster), to see that this relativity goes through all our natural or sense knowledge. It is different with intellectual relations.

such consciousness gives it. Here comes in the mind's own contribution to the world as it knows it—the brightness of light, the gaiety of colour, the melody of sound, the fragrance of odours, delights of the palate, the robing of sensation generally—which is the principal source of its delight and charm to the sentient being. Thus, after all, Locke's distinction of primary and secondary qualities is vindicated, though on a different ground from that on which he placed it.

CHAPTER IX

HUME ON MORALS: UTILITARIANISM

IN the history of ethical systems, three prevailing modes of contemplating the phenomena of morals may be distinguished, each connected with great names, and each still finding its defenders. They may be termed respectively the *Æsthetic*, the *Stoic* or *Jural*, and the *Utilitarian*. The ruling thought in the first class of systems is the Beautiful (τὸ καλόν); in the second, the Right; in the third, the Useful. Plato and Shaftesbury may represent the first; Kant may stand for the second; Hume was an advocate of the third, though not to the exclusion of the first.

Since the time of Hume, the utilitarian philosophy has risen into great prominence in Britain. Fixing on the acknowledged tendency of virtuous acts and dispositions to promote the happiness of the individual and of society, this system erects utility to the place of a universal moral standard, and proclaims it as the one source of moral distinctions. The theory assumes two forms, according as the end contemplated is the happiness of the *individual*, or the happiness of *society* in general. The former is the selfish, the latter the disinterested type of utilitarianism. The system has, however, its natural parent in the ancient

Epicureanism, with its exaltation of pleasure as the chief good; and if the doctrine, in its later form, has received into itself elements in virtue of which it is capable of assuming a more plausible character, it achieves this only by a happy inconsistency.[1] With the rise of the evolutionary philosophy, specially in the hands of Mr. Spencer, the utilitarian hypothesis has undergone radical transformations. This has happened mainly in three respects: (1) in the explanation of moral "intuitions" through the accumulated experiences of the race transmitted by inheritance; (2) in the attempt to deduce the laws of morality directly from the laws of evolution; (3) in modifications of the idea of the moral end in the substitution, *e.g.*, of "efficiency," "life," "health" of the social organism for the older "happiness."[2] Most of these later developments lie beyond our purview, nor does the final confession of the author of the evolutionary mode of treatment lead us to look with much hope to its results.[3]

In this development of the utilitarian philosophy in Britain, Hume's writings take a very important place. In some respects the theory of utility has

[1] So Wundt declares that "the term 'utilitarian' is hardly an adequate substitute for the older term 'eudæmonism'" (*Ethics*, ii. p. 176).

[2] Cf. Mr. Leslie Stephen, *Science of Ethics*.

[3] In the Preface to Parts V. and VI. of his *Ethics* (on "Justice"), Mr Spencer says—"Now that . . . I have succeeded in completing the second volume of *The Principles of Ethics* . . . my satisfaction is somewhat dashed by the thought that the new parts fall short of expectation. . . . The doctrine of evolution has not furnished guidance to the extent I had hoped. Most of the conclusions, drawn empirically, are such as right feelings, enlightened by cultivated intelligence, have already sufficed to establish," etc.

never found a better advocate than it did in him. Hume was not, indeed, the first to lay stress, in the philosophy of morals, on the disinterested affections. Cumberland and Shaftesbury had done that far earlier; and many of Hume's arguments on this head are simple adaptations of those of Hutcheson and Butler. Still, it cannot be doubted that Hume's able advocacy gave a new impetus to the more disinterested form of the theory of utility; and, notwithstanding a partial re-action to the selfish view under Paley, we may trace since his day an increased prevalence of what is called, in utilitarian phraseology, "the greatest happiness principle." Alike in Jeremy Bentham, who is specially identified with this principle,[1] and in James Mill, there is obvious difficulty in adjusting the relations of the two interests, public and private; and justice and benevolence on their theory constantly tend to sink back into more refined forms of self-love. J. S. Mill, however, distinctly enunciates the principle, "The utilitarian standard is not the agent's own greatest happiness, but the greatest amount of happiness altogether."[2] The selfish doctrine of Hobbes and Paley, therefore—the "ethics of interest," as Cousin called it—is thus set aside as defenceless by the best advocates of the theory. To Hume, with his powerful polemic against self-love as the principle of morals, must be attributed part of the credit of this result.

[1] The author of the phrase is really Priestley, who in his *Essay on Government* in 1768 introduced as the proper object of government, "the greatest happiness of the greatest number." Bentham followed in 1776 (the year of Hume's death), adopting the phrase. Mr. Leslie Stephen carries it still further back to Hutcheson (*English Thought*, ii. p. 61).

[2] *Utilitarianism*, p. 24.

But we shall see that the credit has to be qualified in several important ways.

Hume's theory of morals, originally published (1740) as Book III. of the *Treatise on Human Nature*, was, like the first Book, recast, and afterwards published as the *Enquiry concerning the Principles of Morals.* With this work has to be taken the "Dissertation on the Passions," appended to the *Enquiry concerning the Human Understanding*, which corresponds to the original Book II. of the *Treatise.* The "Dissertation" of itself does not contain much that need detain us. It is interesting as an attempt, which in parts reminds of Spinoza, to give not merely a classification of the "passions" (under which Hume includes all appetites, desires, affections, emotions), but as far as possible a *rationale* of them. Occasionally Hume falls back on "original instincts," as when he says of pride, "I find that the peculiar object of pride and humility is determined by an original and natural instinct";[1] and of benevolence, "It is a constitution of nature of which we can give no further explanation."[2] In explaining the passions, he makes use of what he calls "the double relations of ideas and impressions,[3] *e.g.*, both the object of pride and the passion of pride have relation to "self"; again, the object is something agreeable, and the passion is likewise an agreeable feeling. His whole aim he thus sums up at the close: "It is sufficient for my purpose if I have made it appear that in the production and conduct of the passions there is a certain regular mechanism,

[1] Works, ii. p. 16. [2] *Ibid.* iv. pp. 212–13.

[3] *Ibid.* ii. p. 17; cf. iv. p. 216: "The double relations of sentiments and ideas." The discussion is intricate and confusing.

which is susceptible of as accurate a disquisition, as the laws of motion, optics, hydrostatics, or any part of natural philosophy."[1] Which "accurate disquisition," assuredly, Hume's "Dissertation" has not approved itself to be.

Hume's determination in his "Dissertation" to know nothing but impressions and ideas in arbitrary conjunction, involves him in curious paradoxes. What could be odder, *e.g.*, than his contention that "if nature had so pleased, love might have had the same effect as hatred, and hatred as love. I see no contradiction in supposing a desire of producing misery annexed to love, and of happiness to hatred."[2] Occasionally, too, under the influence of his defective psychology, we find him slipping into such confusions of intellectual and emotional phenomena as the following: "What is commonly, in a popular sense, called reason . . . is nothing but a calm passion which takes a comprehensive and a distinct view of its object, and actuates the will without any sensible emotion."[3] It would be easy to show that, nevertheless, the "Dissertation" involves many principles, which, if pushed, would be fatal to his main doctrine. His whole theory of pride and humility, *e.g.*, turns on the possession of that idea of "self" which, in his theoretic philosophy, he had demonstrated could not exist, since we have no "impression" of it. How, again, in the light of his first principles, are we to construe such a sentence as the following?—

"Being so far advanced as to observe a difference

[1] Works, iv. p. 226.

[2] *Ibid.* ii. p. 112.

[3] *Ibid.* iv. p. 220. One is reminded of the Hobbean notion of contemplative and reasoning passions.

between the *object* of the passions and their *cause*, and to distinguish in the cause the *quality which operates* on the passions, from the *subject* in which it *inheres*, we now proceed," etc.[1]

It is, however, only with the bearings of the "Dissertation" on the theory of morals we are at present concerned, and here its principal interest lies in the opening positions on *Good* and *Evil*, and on the relations of our desires and emotions to these. Hume's theory on this subject is, in brief, precisely that of Hobbes and Locke, viz., that Good and Evil are but names for pleasure and pain respectively.

"Some objects," he says, "produce immediately an agreeable sensation, by the original structure of our organs, and are thence denominated GOOD; as others, from their immediately disagreeable sensations, acquire the appellation EVIL. . . . Some objects, again, by being naturally conformable or contrary to passion, excite an agreeable or painful sensation; and are thence called *Good* or *Evil*."[2]

When good or evil is certain, or very probable, there arises, in the one case JOY, in the other GRIEF or SORROW; when the good or evil is uncertain, it gives rise to HOPE or FEAR.

"DESIRE arises from good, considered simply, and AVERSION from evil. The WILL exerts itself, when either the presence of the good, or absence of the evil, may be attained by any action of the mind or body."[3]

That is to say, good and evil, which awaken desire and aversion, and alone can set the will in motion, are

[1] Works, ii. p. 9. Only some of the italics are Hume's.

[2] *Ibid.* iv. p. 189. Cf. Locke's *Essay*, bk. ii. ch. 20.

[3] *Ibid.* iv. pp. 190–1; cf. ii. p. 353.

agreeable or *disagreeable sensations*, or personal pleasure and pain. The effect of this initial doctrine on the theory of morals can readily be anticipated.

We return now to the *Enquiry* in its connection with the *Treatise*. A comparison of these two shows that, if the earlier work is somewhat rough and unsystematic, it is nevertheless the more vigorous exposition of Hume's ideas. The *Enquiry*, however, is the more polished and readable. In it the doctrine of utility as the foundation of morals is more distinctly expounded. It has been mentioned that Hume himself regarded it as the best of his works, and perhaps it is, if judged by a purely literary standard. It has at least this merit, that its drift is not, like some of his other works, sceptical and destructive. Hume has reached the smooth waters of the "easy" philosophy, and avows himself as on the side of "common sense and reason," as against those "disingenuous disputants" who "have denied the reality of moral distinctions"![1]

In the *Enquiry*, as in the *Treatise*, Hume begins by considering the question of "the general foundation of morals; whether they be derived from reason or sentiment";[2] and, after weighing the matter *pro* and *con.*, he concludes that both have to do with our moral decisions. Reason is required to sift the facts, and make the proper distinctions, exclusions, and com-

[1] Works, iv. p. 229. His own speculations *do* tend to take the foundation from morality, *e.g.*, in his "Dialogue" on moral distinctions (Works, iv. pp. 395 ff.). In a letter to Hutcheson he wishes he could "avoid concluding" that morality, as determined by sentiment, is something quite relative to humanity (Burton, i. pp. 119–20).

[2] *Ibid.* iv. p. 231.

parisons;[1] but he thinks it probable that "the final sentence depends on some internal sense or feeling which nature has made universal in the whole species."[2] For the better determination of this question, he proposes to analyse "that complication of mental qualities which form what, in common life, we term *Personal Merit*."[3] The method by which he proceeds is that of an induction of particular instances. His only object, he assures us, "is to discover the circumstances on both sides which are common to the estimable and blamable qualities, to observe that particular in which the estimable qualities agree on the one hand, and the blamable on the other; and thence to reach the foundation of ethics, and find those universal principles from which all censure or approbation is ultimately derived."[4] We shall have occasion to notice that in Hume's treatment of morals, he deals almost entirely with the estimable and blamable qualities of the *agent*, scarcely ever with the abstract morality of the *act*. In this respect his system constitutes a curious contrast to the doctrine of later utilitarians, who give chief prominence to the *morality of the action*. The purpose of utilitarianism, Mr. Mill tells us, is to show what actions are right and what wrong, irrespective of the character or feelings from which they spring.[5]

We have already anticipated the result of Hume's proof. It leads him to conclude in favour of *public utility* as the mark and test of virtuous qualities and dispositions.[6]

[1] It will be observed how a distinguishing, judging, comparing reason is constantly assumed.

[2] Works, iv. p. 233. It is shown below that this "sense" is not after all regarded as original.

[3] *Ibid.* iv. p. 234. [4] *Ibid.* iv. p. 235. [5] *Utilit.* p. 29.

[6] As early as 1739 we find him writing to Hutcheson, "Now I desire

"The necessity of justice (to Hume an 'artificial' virtue) to the support of society is the SOLE foundation of that virtue; and since no moral excellence is more highly esteemed, we may conclude that this circumstance of usefulness has, in general, the strongest energy, and most entire command over our sentiments. It must therefore be the source of a considerable part of the merit ascribed to humanity, benevolence, friendship, public spirit, and other social virtues of that stamp: as it is the SOLE source of the moral approbation paid to fidelity, justice, veracity, integrity, and those other estimable and useful qualities and principles. It is entirely agreeable to the rules of philosophy, and even of common reason, where any principle has been found to have a great force and energy in one instance, to ascribe to it a like energy in all similar instances. This indeed is Newton's chief rule of philosophising."[1]

This conclusion, indeed, is not drawn with great logical strictness. In regard to benevolence, for example, he claims to have proved no more than that the utility resulting from the social virtues forms at least *a part* of their merit,[2] and he sums up thus:—

"It appears to be a matter of fact that the circumstance of *utility*, in all subjects, is a source of praise and approbation; that it is constantly appealed to in all moral decisions concerning the merit and demerit of actions; that it is the *sole* source of that high regard paid to justice, fidelity, honour, allegiance, and chastity; that it is inseparable from all the other

you to consider if there be any quality that is virtuous, without having a tendency either to the public good or to the good of the person who possesses it," etc. (Burton, i. p. 115).

[1] Works, iv. p. 267. [2] *Ibid.* iv. p. 243.

social virtues, humanity, generosity, charity, affability, levity, mercy, and moderation; and, in a word, it is a foundation of the *chief part* of morals, which has a reference to mankind and our fellow creatures."[1]

The reason of the important qualification which Hume here makes proves to be that, besides the quality of *usefulness* to ourselves and others, he recognises the quality of *agreeableness* to ourselves and others, as a ground of moral approbation. In his formal statements he always joins together "useful and agreeable": the *utile* and the *dulce*.[2] The distinction may at first sight not seem to be great, but by *useful* Hume has in view qualities directed to ends other than themselves; by *agreeable*, qualities which give immediate satisfaction to their possessors or to others. Such are cheerfulness, greatness of mind, courage, tranquillity, in the former class; politeness, wit, decorum, in the latter. The fault of such a classification is obvious, since, as was objected at the time, (1) it confounds talents and accomplishments with virtues, and (2) overlooks that mere "agreeableness" is far from constituting virtue. Beauty of person, *e.g.*, is an agreeable quality to its possessor, but is not a virtue. It is more important to notice that, in Hume's view, the qualities in question are adjudged to be virtues, not from the standpoint of their possessors, but from that of the *sympathetic onlooker*. The cheerful man's state of mind may be a gratification to himself, but it is the sympathetic pleasure felt in it by the disinterested observer which contributes the element of *approbation*.[3] Of course qualities that are agreeable can be also useful, and qualities that are useful, *e.g.*,

[1] Works, iv. p. 295. [2] *Ibid.* iv. p. 335. [3] Cf. *ibid.* ii. pp. 372–3.

benevolence, are likewise agreeable in themselves. Hence the *other* part of the merit ascribed to benevolence.[1]

The next question relates to the *nature* of the *moral sentiment*, and this Hume discusses chiefly under the heading, "Why Utility Pleases." It cannot be affirmed that his doctrine on the point is either clear or satisfactory. We have found him declaring above, in accordance with "the elegant Shaftesbury" and with Hutcheson, that it is probable that the final sentence in morals "depends on some internal sense or feeling which nature has made universal in the whole species."[2] Similarly in the *Treatise*, "moral distinctions" are held to be "derived from a moral sense."[3]

"An action, or sentiment, or character, is virtuous or vicious: why? Because its view causes a pleasure or uneasiness of a particular kind. In giving a reason, therefore, for the pleasure or uneasiness, we sufficiently explain the vice or virtue. To have the sense of virtue, is nothing but to *feel* a satisfaction of a particular kind from the contemplation of a character. The very *feeling* constitutes our praise or admiration. We can go no further; nor do we inquire into the cause of the satisfaction."[4]

It is natural to presume that, as with the writers above named, this "internal sense" is regarded as an

[1] "As love is *immediately agreeable* to the person who is actuated by it, and hatred *immediately disagreeable*, this may also be a considerable reason why we praise all the passions that partake of the former, and blame all those that have any considerable share of the latter. . . . All this seems to me a proof that our approbation has, in these cases, an origin different from the prospect of utility and advantage, either to ourselves or others" (Works, ii. p. 388).

[2] Works, iv. p. 233; cf. p. 356.

[3] See above, p. 173.

[4] *Ibid.* ii. p. 233; cf. pp. 231, 238, 354.

original principle of human nature. As we proceed, however, we make the discovery that it is not so. We have not gone far before we find our author departing from the underived "moral sense" of Shaftesbury and Hutcheson, and identifying the principle of approval and disapproval with the sentiment of benevolence, humanity, or generous sympathy. *This* is "Why Utility Pleases." We are constituted to take pleasure in the happiness of others, to sympathise with them, to seek their good. This leads us to look with complacency on all acts and qualities that tend to this end, as on the end itself. "It is impossible for such a creature as man to be wholly indifferent to the well- or ill-being of his fellow-creatures, and not readily of himself to pronounce . . . that what promotes their happiness is good, what tends to their misery is evil."[1] It is not, therefore, acts useful to ourselves, but acts useful to others, or to society as a whole, we approve of.

"Thus in whatever light we take this subject, the merit ascribed to the social virtues appears still uniform, and arises chiefly from that regard which the natural sentiment of benevolence engages us to pay to the interests of mankind and society."[2]

"The notion of morals implies some sentiment common to all mankind, which recommends the same object to general approbation, and makes every man, or most men, agree in the same opinion or decision concerning it. It also implies some sentiment, so universal and comprehensive, as to extend to all mankind, and render the actions and conduct, even of the persons the most remote, an object of applause or censure, according as they agree or disagree with that

[1] Works, iv. p. 294. [2] *Ibid.*

rule of right which is established. These two requisite circumstances belong alone to the sentiment of humanity here insisted on."[1]

One curious result of this derivation of moral sentiment entirely from benevolence, is that the theory of Hume, like that of Hutcheson, would seem to have no room left in it for duties to self. It fails to give any reason why conscience should smile approval on a man for any act tending to *his own good.* It was probably in view of this defect, and with the purpose of meeting it, that Adam Smith developed his peculiar doctrine of reflex sympathy. It is the more interesting, therefore, to observe that Hume, in his earlier work, has already anticipated this objection, and given an explanation which is almost identical with Smith's,—which probably, indeed, furnished the latter with the germ of his peculiar theory. The close of the following passage illustrates this. The point of Adam Smith's theory, it may be remembered, is, that the individual's approbation of merit in himself arises from sympathy with the approval of the disinterested spectator—a sufficiently roundabout hypothesis. So Hume says:—

"Nay, when the injustice is so distant from us as in no way to affect our interest, it still displeases us; because we consider it as prejudicial to human society, and pernicious to every one that approaches the person guilty of it. We partake of their uneasiness by *sympathy;* and as everything that gives uneasiness in human actions, upon the general survey, is called vice, and whatever produces satisfaction, in the same manner, is denominated virtue, this is the reason why the sense of moral good and evil follows upon justice

[1] Works, ii. p. 339.

and injustice. And though this sense, in the present case, be derived only from contemplating the actions of others, yet we fail not to extend it even to our own actions. The *general rule* reaches beyond these instances from which it arose; while, at the same time, we naturally sympathise with others in the sentiments they entertain of us." [1]

Apart from deeper criticism, the obvious remark to be made on this view is, that mere sympathy with the agreeable experiences of others, whatever pleasure it may yield us, is a very different sentiment from that of moral approbation. It is far from true that everything which excites "uneasiness" in human actions, on a survey of them, is called "vice," or that which produces satisfaction, "virtue"; else our sympathy with the feelings of a criminal about to be hanged might lead to a condemnation of the act which sentenced him. The acts must be of the kind we judge *moral*, before the feelings we call approbation or disapprobation can arise, and the feelings are regulated by the character of our judgment. This was another defect in Hume's doctrine which Adam Smith attempted to supply by his doctrine of "propriety." A deeper question will arise immediately as to the origin of the disinterested sentiment itself.

To complete this view of Hume's doctrine, we have still to consider another point necessarily brought up in all discussions of moral subjects—the idea or feeling of *obligation*. Here, most of all, the theory of Hume, and utilitarian systems generally, are felt to be deficient. The question is, Why am I *bound* to perform certain actions rather than others? What constitutes the

[1] Works, ii. p. 266; cf. p. 373.

oughtness which I feel in regard to them? Butler answers by an appeal to the authority of conscience; Kant, by an appeal to the "categorical imperative" of moral law. But Hume and Mill have no answer to give based on a moral demand which carries with it its own authority. Hume in particular can hardly be said to have faced the question at all; he rather adroitly avoids it, and substitutes another in its place. "Having explained the moral approbation attending merit or virtue, there remains nothing but briefly to consider our interested *obligation* to it, and to inquire whether every man, who has any regard to his own happiness or welfare, will not best find his account in the practice of every moral duty."[1]

The object of this concluding section, accordingly, is to show "that all the duties which it (the foregoing system) recommends are also the true interest of each individual."[2] Obligation, in other words, is simply, on this doctrine, another name for the selfish impulse. Here surely is the truth coming out at last! In whatever the rightness of an action was placed, it might have seemed evident that the *obligation* to perform it was *something which flowed from that rightness*, and needed nothing else to account for it. I *ought* to do the action because I see it to be *right*. But Hume has placed the rightness of actions on the ground of their conduciveness to the public benefit. And this consideration of utility will not yield the consciousness of obligation. Hence he is compelled in the last resort to identify obligation with self-interest. I *ought* to do a thing because it is for *my own good*.[3] This is a return

[1] Works, iv. p. 346. [2] *Ibid.* iv. p. 348.

[3] In another place, in speaking of political justice, he says "the

to precisely that selfish view of morals which he had previously rejected. It implies that a stronger motive than the simple goodness of the action is required to make a moral agent feel his obligation, and that self-interest is the strongest motive which can be brought to bear upon him. Only, unfortunately, when it *is* brought to bear upon him, it is *not* the motive of moral obligation. Between that motive and the consideration of self-interest, there is a world of difference.

The thing chiefly important to notice in this connection is, that this is no accidental flaw in Hume's theory, or in any theory of the kind; it springs from its essential nature. Starting from Hume's principle (which was that of Hobbes, Locke, and of nearly all moral speculators before him), that the Good—the sole object of desire, that which ultimately moves the will, and alone can finally move it—is *pleasure*, no other conclusion is possible than that which Hume reaches. It might be shown that the sentimental moralists, even those who lay most stress on the benevolent affections, necessarily fall into the same snare; finding, as they must, the ultimate sanction of morality in a *state of feeling*, viz., the peculiar pleasure yielded by the moral sense. This is true of Shaftesbury, who labours to establish that "to have the natural affections (such as are founded in Love, Complacency, and Good-will, and in a sympathy with the kind or species) is to have the chief means and power of self-enjoyment; and that to want them is certain misery and ill";[1] of Hutcheson, who thinks that any fear of sacrifice of

moral obligation holds proportion with the usefulness" (Works, iv. p. 269). He should rather say "with the self-interest."

[1] *Inquiry concerning Virtue*, i. 2. 1; cf. ii. 1. 3.

individual happiness must be removed, "if we have a moral sense and public affections, whose gratifications are constituted by nature our most intense and durable pleasures";[1] of even Butler, who strangely declares that "when we sit down in a cool hour we can neither justify to ourselves this or that pursuit, till we are convinced that it will be for our happiness, or at least not contrary to it."[2] Hume's position is quite identical. "Each person loves himself better than any other single person. . . . It appears that, in the original frame of our mind, our strongest attention is confined to ourselves; our next is extended to our relatives and acquaintance," etc.[3] Nay, ere long it comes to be seen that there is an inconsistency in the admission of purely disinterested affections at all. However strongly their existence is affirmed, the necessity of the case tends to an explanation of them which finds their origin in egoistic principles. That Hume should derive justice from the selfish impulse in man, is comprehensible;[4] but in addition to this, there are attempts even to give a *rationale* of sympathy of a kind which robs it of its primary disinterested character. E.g.:—

"The minds of all men are similar in their feelings and operations; nor can any one be actuated by any affection of which all others are not in some degree susceptible. As in strings equally wound up, the motion of one communicates itself to the rest, so all the affections readily pass from one person to another, and beget correspondent movements in every human

[1] *On Passions and Affections*, p. 19.

[2] *Sermons*, xi. Cf. Sorley's *Ethics of Naturalism*, p. 88.

[3] Works, ii. p. 252–3.

[4] *Ibid.* ii. p. 355.

creature. . . . When I perceive the causes of any emotion, my mind is conveyed to its effects, and is actuated by a like emotion. . . . No passion of another discovers itself immediately to the mind. We are only sensible of its causes or effects. From *these* we infer the passion; and consequently *these* give rise to our sympathy."[1] Sympathy is thus a sort of automatic process, by which pains or pleasures similar to those we witness are reproduced in ourselves.

"When any quality or character has a tendency to the good of mankind, we are pleased with it, and approve of it, because it presents the lively idea of pleasure; which idea affects us by sympathy, and is itself a kind of pleasure."[2]

It is the case, accordingly, that in the utilitarian schools which succeeded Hume, the egoistic genesis of even benevolent sentiments is frankly recognised,[3] and the motive of self-interest is invariably fallen back on as the ground of obligation. The representatives of these schools saw, indeed, that Hume's theory needed supplementing. They recognised, what he did not, that obligation has reference, not immediately to self-interest, but to *law* and *authority*. If men were left merely to consult what they considered their own interests in relation to moral action, society would soon fall to pieces. There is a necessity for an outward check or constraint. The law of the State, therefore, and the force of public opinion, are the great elements in what Mr. Mill calls "the external sanction

[1] Works, ii. p. 355. [2] *Ibid.* ii. p. 361.

[3] Not by every one so frankly as Bentham, when he wrote: "I am a selfish man, as selfish as any man can be. But in me, somehow or other, so it happens, selfishness has taken the shape of benevolence."

of virtue.[1] But clearly this is still an utterly inadequate account of obligation. *Enforced obedience* is no true obedience in the moral sense. It is only when we feel the law to be *right* that we regard ourselves as under real obligation to perform it. This is virtually admitted by Mr. Mill when he says: "It is part of the notion of duty that a man may be *rightfully* compelled to perform it." When the man perceives this *right* in the compulsion, the obligation is already transferred to another sphere. Mr. Mill, however, lays comparatively little stress on the *external* sanction, as compared with what he calls the *internal* sanction. We question whether, after all, he has thereby approached much nearer the solution of the problem. This "internal sanction" is derived from our social feelings, combined with education, association, and elements derived from other sources, to which the evolutionary school would add the accumulated results of inheritance. The binding force then consists, Mr. Mill would tell us, in the "mass of feeling" which must be broken through in order to violate that standard of right, and which, if we do violate it, will have to be encountered in the specific form of *remorse*. But why of *remorse?* Granted a nucleus of original moral ideas, around which the mass of associated feelings gathers, we can understand the peculiar nature of the compound, but not otherwise. An accumulation of feelings, none of them originally moral, can hardly, by any chemistry of association, develop features so marked and unique as those of the moral sentiments. Has this "mass of feeling" no moral elements in the heart of it? Or is it something to which we must

[1] So also Bentham, Austin, and James Mill.

perforce submit because we cannot now shake off its power? Then it ceases to be obligation the moment a man, from any cause, feels strong enough to break from its yoke. Even on the evolutionist hypothesis that the feelings have influence, because in them is registered the experience of the race as to what is best for its "life," "efficiency," or "well-being," this alone does not suffice to constitute obligation. The individual has still to be brought to perceive the reasonableness and duty of subordinating his individual will, it may be of sacrificing his personal interest, to that which is best for the good of the whole.

This brings us to the really crucial point in the judgment of Hume's and similar theories—the true nature of the *moral end.* Is it pleasure, in Hume's sense of "agreeable sensation"? Or is it something higher—say the realisation of man's complete nature in the due subordination of its power and capacities —the attainment, not of happiness in the sense of "a sum of pleasures," but of "perfection," which brings with it, indeed, the purest pleasures, but only as delight and satisfaction in the things which are esteemed the true goods of the soul, among which the pure heart, the upright will, the wise mind, the social affections, will take the highest rank? It should by this time be a truth so well understood as to need no vindication, that happiness in the true sense—as real satisfaction of the self—is not to be found by direct seeking of it, but only by devotion to ends *other* than happiness—ends having value in themselves—in the pursuit and attainment of which happiness comes. But the subject requires a deeper elucidation.

To test this theory, then, let us start with its root-conception—that of Hobbes, Locke, Bentham, Mill, even of Mr. Spencer,[1] as well as of Hume—that *good* is merely a synonym for *pleasure*. A first question here might be: Is this even a *possible* end for a rational being, not to say for one seeking to live rationally? Pleasure is a state of simple *feeling*, and of *individual* feeling. But a rational being is one who, in virtue of his reason, has passed beyond mere feeling, has risen above it, has constituted for himself relations with his fellow-men, and a "realm of ends," in which his higher self and its interests have expressed themselves; who is the subject of desires, ambitions, aims, which only thought could originate, and a self-conscious agent experience. The self of the rational being is thus immensely larger than his egoistic self: takes in a world of persons and interests that lie beyond his narrow personal horizon. It is in the nature of things impossible, therefore, that such a being should not set before him ends other and higher than pleasure. But even if it *were* possible to make pleasure the sole end, a next question would be: Is a life which has only pleasure for its end one *worthy* of a rational being? If he stoops to make pleasure his sole end, is he not consciously degrading and impoverishing himself? It can only be maintained that he is not, if there are no higher ends to which his rational and spiritual nature points him; and this we explicitly deny to be the case.

The answer that will be given to this kind of reasoning naturally will be, that we are playing upon an

[1] Cf. *Data of Ethics*, p. 27. The question of optimism is declared to be simply that of "a surplus of pleasurable feeling over painful feeling" (pp. 29–30).

ambiguity in the word "pleasure"; are using it in the sense of mere animal gratification; whereas the utilitarian, it will be held, has in view the whole scale of pleasures from lowest to highest, and, equally with others, discriminates between their values. It is not strictly the case that all utilitarians do this (Mr. Bentham for one did not); some, however, as J. S. Mill, have done so, but thereby have only introduced into the system a new inconsistency. For obviously, as soon as we have introduced the element of *quality* into pleasures, we raise a new question,—that of the standard or ideal. How else are we to determine which pleasures are *high* and which *low;* which men ought to choose, and which they ought to despise and reject? Reflection will show that, in another respect, whenever we introduce the idea of *scale* into pleasures, the problem is entirely changed. The pleasures we place higher in the scale—intellectual pleasures, *e.g.*, or moral pleasures—cease to be *mere* pleasures; they are results, reflexes, accompaniments, of the higher energies which give rise to them, and they derive their dignity and excellence solely from these. It is the objects of the energies which are the ends, not the pleasures. Take the case of benevolence—the disinterested seeking of another's welfare. This is in a sense the foundation of Hume's whole theory; it is the more strange that he did not perceive how, instead of being an instance of the seeking of pleasure as one's only good, it is, in its very nature, a refutation of that principle. Pleasure, in the nature of the case, is the pleasure of the person *experiencing* it, not of the person *conferring* it, or of the mere *spectator.* The well-doer may derive pleasure from his benevolence, or from seeing the happiness of others; but that pleasure is not the motive of his action. The good to which his action is directed is not his own good, but the good of another. Pleasure, in the sense of an "agreeable sensation" *to him*, is not his end, not the thing he desires, or which moves his will. To resolve the motive of benevolence into the pleasure derived from it by the doer, is to deny its disinterested character, and reduce it to a finer form of selfishness. But in respect even of the person benefited, must it be "pleasure" only which I desire for him? If my own well-being includes higher ends, why should his not do so also? If I regard a disinterested habit of soul as a good for myself, it cannot but be that I shall desire it for others as well, and include it also in my ideal of the "well-being" of society. What is now said of benevolence applies to all the higher desires which intelligence goes to constitute—desire of knowledge, desire of society, desire of power, desire of property, etc. The pleasures arising from these desires are no longer *mere* pleasures. They are accompaniments of energies directed to ends which are esteemed to be of worth for themselves, and *hence* beget pleasure.

Finally, the question may be brought to the test of fact. Is it the case that all men do set happiness, in the sense of pleasure, before them as their highest end, and the only thing desirable? For this is what Hume and all utilitarians assume. We recall here, in the first place, a remark of Mr. Mill's own: "It is better to be a Socrates dissatisfied than a fool satisfied."[1] We notice, secondly, the admission of all the higher class of utilitarians, that virtue ought to become an end,

[1] *Utilitarianism*, p. 14.

and to be loved for its own sake. "The mind," says Mr. Mill, "is not in a right state, nor in a state conformable to utility, not in a state most conducive to the general happiness, unless it does love virtue in this manner, as a thing desirable in itself."[1] This, it must be felt, is a very remarkable position. The utilitarian tells us, in the first instance, that the rightness, the goodness, of actions lies only in their conduciveness to happiness; yet we are informed that it is right and even necessary that men should come to believe in virtue as having a goodness and value in itself. Why it should be advantageous that men should come under this delusion is not very obvious. It seems like saying that, however true utilitarianism may be, it is not desirable that men should believe in it; that, practically, it is necessary that they should act on another hypothesis. But, thirdly, without dwelling on this, are there not numberless cases in which we judge that we ought to do a certain action for far higher reasons than merely that it conduces to happiness? Hume regards justice as resting wholly on human convention; but are there not judgments in the sphere of justice which arise prior to, and independently of, all human sanction? When, for instance, we reflect that we ought to be fair and candid in our dealings with others *even in our thoughts*, is there no motive except that such fairness and candour will be preeminently useful to society? Do we not feel that it would be *in itself* an unworthy thing to act otherwise; unworthy of our own character and dignity as rational and moral beings? Do we not recognise that we ought to respect the rights of others, as Kant would say,

[1] *Utilitarianism*, p. 56.

for the sake of the humanity that is in them? Are we not bound to respect their liberty, their consciences, their intelligence, their possessions lawfully acquired, on the simple grounds that they are *persons?* For the same reason every man owes a certain respect to *himself*, and is bound to use every means to conserve and perfect his nature. Those qualities, *e.g.*, which Hume specifies as useful or agreeable to one's self—self-control, magnanimity, tranquillity, and the like—shall we say that it is their utility or agreeableness which is the ground on which we pronounce them virtues? *Why* do we praise them? Is it not because we discern in them an intrinsic excellence? And is not their "agreeableness" to us simply the index and result of this high esteem in which we hold them? When Kant says, "There is nothing in the world which can be termed absolutely and altogether good, a good will alone excepted,"[1] do we not feel instinctively the nobility of his utterance, and recognise that *such* a possession is more desirable than any amount of "pleasure"? It may be true—though it is far from being always the case—that the highest dignity and integrity of a nature brings with it also the greatest happiness; but the happiness assuredly is not the first thing aimed at. The man who would barter his integrity for any increase of pleasure has no true integrity to barter.

There is no coldness in Hume's praises of virtue, though it is rather the "beauty" and "amiability" of moral qualities than the character of acts as "right" and "wrong" that engage his interest. But the defect in his foundation weakens his whole structure, and

[1] *Met. of Ethics*, ch. i.

leaves him with no room for "duty for duty's sake." Everything becomes precarious because based simply on the pleasing and customary. This is seen in the easy view he takes of male chastity, and in his defence of the right of suicide. There is no place for heroic virtue of any kind in Hume. His ethics, as Mr. Green remarked, never rise above the level of "respectability." Language like Wordsworth's in his "Ode to Duty," or such as Carlyle's on the eternal and infinite difference between right and wrong, would sound meaningless to him. Even Justice in his hands sinks down to mere human "artifice." As for the higher obligations and sanctions of religion, these, it is needless to say, altogether disappear.

CHAPTER X

Hume and Theology: Miracles

After metaphysics, there is perhaps no sphere in which Hume's influence has been so palpably felt as in theology. Hume is not, as we shall immediately see, to be off-hand classed with English deists or French atheists. His speculations went much deeper than those of either. On the one hand, he always professed, however inconsistently, some kind of belief in a Supreme Being; on the other, his philosophy was as fatal to the natural revelation of Deism as it was to the supernatural revelation of Christianity. His arguments, a little altered, have passed into the camp of unbelief, and taken a permanent place in its armoury. It is significant that nearly every modern theorist on the subject of religion — deist, pantheist, agnostic, pessimist, believer in a limited God, and believer in no God at all—can find his share in Hume, and fortify himself by his reasonings.

It was remarked in the Introduction, that in Hume, as in some of his contemporaries, the sense for religion appears almost entirely wanting. He tells Sir William Elliot, indeed, *à propos* of the *Dialogues concerning Natural Religion*, that he began his inquiries with a search for arguments to confirm the common opinion, but that gradually doubts "stole in."[1] That stage, however, if it ever existed to any marked extent, was prehistoric in Hume's career; it antecedes any definite knowledge we have of him. It is certain, as before hinted, that at a very early period he had reasoned himself out of all positive beliefs in respect of religion, and had betaken himself for his ideals of life to his two favourites, Cicero and Virgil. The influences of French literature and society were not likely to do much towards the removal of this antipathy; and it is to be feared that his personal disposition—his easy temper, his love of fame, his engrained sceptical habit—made him naturally averse from any system which identified itself with earnest faith, or intensity of moral purpose.

It contributed to this aversion that the age in which Hume lived was one marked by a cold, rationalising temper generally. The account he gives in one of his Essays of the state of religion in his time recalls a well-known passage in Butler:—

"Most people in this Island," he says, "have divested themselves of all superstitious reverence to names and authority; the clergy have lost much of their credit, their pretensions and doctrines have been ridiculed; and even religion can scarcely support itself in the world."[2]

[1] Burton, i. p. 332. See above, p. 47.

[2] Works, iii. p. 51. Butler's statement in the Advertisement to the first edition of his *Analogy* is: "It is come, I know not how, to be taken for granted, by many persons, that Christianity is not so much as a subject of inquiry; but that it is, now at length, discovered to be fictitious. And accordingly they treat it as if, in the present age, this were an agreed point among all people of discernment; and nothing remained, but to set it up as a principal subject of mirth and ridicule, as it were by way of reprisals, for its having so long interrupted the pleasures of the world."

It never enters Hume's mind to doubt that morals, politics, social life, could go on quite well without religion; on the contrary, he has a firm persuasion that things would be better in its absence. Philo's words in the *Dialogues* may be assumed to be a true expression of his own sentiments on this point:—

"If the religious spirit be ever mentioned in any historical narration, we are sure to meet afterwards with a detail of the miseries which attend it. And no period of time can be happier or more prosperous than those in which it is never regarded or heard of."[1]

Naturally, with such views, repugnance to everything savouring of "priesthood" was one of the strongest passions of Hume's nature; and his customary synonym for religion was "enthusiasm" or "fanaticism." No doubt all this is spoken of the religion of the "vulgar," or "religion as it has commonly been found in the world,"[2] and exception is made, as we shall find, of the "philosophical" religion, which resolves itself into the "speculative tenet of Theism,"[3] and is admittedly the possession only of a few. But the poverty of Hume's conception of religion generally is manifest in nearly every line he wrote about it. No man, *e.g.*, who ever really understood what true religion is, could have written as he did in the Essay on Immortality:—

"But if any purpose of nature be clear, we may affirm that the whole scope and intention of man's creation, so far as we can judge by natural reason, is limited to the present life. . . . There arise, indeed, in some minds some unaccountable terrors with regard to futurity; but these would quickly vanish were they

[1] Works, ii. p. 530. [2] *Ibid.* ii. p. 534. [3] *Ibid.*

not artificially fostered by precept and example. And those who foster them, what is their motive? Only to gain a livelihood, and to acquire power and riches in this world. Their very zeal and industry, therefore, are an argument against them."[1]

It will not be questioned that Hume's philosophical principles were such as readily lent themselves to the purposes of the religious sceptic, and Hume was by no means slow to make the application. His system had undermined the foundations of all certitude, and, harmless though he might esteem this to be in the common affairs of life, the case was different when it came to questions of religion. His aim here avowedly was "to subvert that abstruse philosophy and metaphysical jargon which, being mixed up with popular superstition, renders it in a manner impenetrable to careless reasoners, and gives it the air of superior wisdom."[2] This could readily be accomplished by a system which grounded all our knowledge and beliefs on sense-experiences. Our inferences may be valid for practical purposes within the circle of experience, but we have no guarantee that they are so beyond it. Hence all questions are at once ruled out which relate to God,[3] the origin of the world, providence, destiny, and the future life. How far Hume meant to include Christianity among his "popular superstitions," may be gathered from other parts of his writings. The Essay on Miracles is a bold attempt to reduce Christianity, as respects its historical foundations, to a tissue of fables, believable only by those who are willing to part with their reason. "Our most holy

[1] Works, iv. p. 549. [2] *Ibid.* iv. p. 9.
[3] On Hume's concessions to Theism, see below.

religion," he says, "is founded on *Faith,* not Reason, and it is a sure method of exposing it to put it to such a trial as it is by no means fitted to bear."[1] We may conjecture how much "faith" Hume would be prepared to concede to a system against which reason was in arms. This mocking deference to a religion in which he had no particle of real belief, is one of the most offensive features in his writings—the adding, if that were possible, of insult to injury.[2] In the Essay on Parties he takes an opportunity of showing in what esteem he held the system here denominated "our most holy religion." Christianity is there represented as a "sect" which owed its success to certain accidental circumstances, and the result of which has been to the world "the greatest misery and devastation." The "furious persecutions of Christianity," he traces, for the most part, to "the imprudent zeal and bigotry of the first propagators of the sect."[3] Of *good* effects resulting from Christianity there is no mention. It is no real contradiction of this, though a fact curious in itself, that, as a concession to the prejudices of the "vulgar," Hume was willing to have an established

[1] Works, iv. p. 149.

[2] Prof. Huxley says: "If ever he seems insincere, it is when he wishes to insult theologians by a parade of sarcastic respect" (*Hume*, p. 140). This, however, was a characteristic feature of the kind of literature which Hume represents. Gibbon's "irony" is proverbial. Shaftesbury indulges profusely in this kind of sarcasm. Rejecting every article of the Christian faith, he professes "his steady orthodoxy, resignation, and entire submission to the truly Christian and Catholic doctrines of our Holy Church, *as by law established.*" On miracles he "submits most willingly, and with full confidence and trust, to the opinions *by law established*" (*Miscell. Reflections*, ii. chs. ii. and iii.). Hume, to his credit, never went so far as that.

[3] Works, iii. p. 61.

Church, on the Presbyterian model too, in his ideal commonwealth.[1] His establishment was meant as a *curb* on religious enthusiasm, not as a means of promoting religion, save of the "philosophical" sort. As Mr. Leslie Stephen says of Shaftesbury: "The Church was excellent as a national refrigerator; but no cultivated person could believe in its doctrines."[2]

In looking at Hume's positions more in detail, we have first to seek to make clear to ourselves his attitude to Theism. We may begin with his *Natural History of Religion*, which was published in his lifetime. This production, which it would not be unjust to describe as a daring piece of satire, yet with a definite enough purpose in the heart of it, forms an essential part of Hume's system. For, even if it be granted that the idea of the supernatural is an illusion, the belief is still at least there as a psychological fact to be accounted for. There are two questions, we are told, to be considered in relation to religion: (1) concerning its foundation in *Human Reason;* and (2) concerning its origin in *Human Nature.*

"Happily," says the sceptic, "the former question, which is the more important, admits of the most obvious, at least the clearest solution. The whole frame of nature bespeaks an Intelligent Author; and no rational inquirer can, after serious reflection, suspend

[1] Works, iii. p. 554. It was essential to Hume's scheme that the Church should be entirely under the control of the magistrates. "The magistrates name rectors or ministers to all the parishes." "The magistrates may take any cause from this (ecclesiastical) court, and determine of themselves." "The magistrates may try, and depose or suspend any presbyter." Thus Hnme's boasted liberality turns round into the sheerest tyranny.

[2] *English Thought in the Eighteenth Century*, ii. p. 19.

his belief for a moment with regard to the primary principles of genuine Theism and Religion."[1]

We are apt to suspect that here again we are on the track of sarcasm; and the rest of the treatise shows us that beyond doubt we are. The direct purpose of the work is to prove that in reality the belief in God and in supernatural existences had a very different origin, viz., in men's ignorance and superstitious fears. Religion has no basis in the essential nature of man—"springs not from an original instinct or primary impression of nature," but arises from "secondary principles[2]—mainly from man's hopes and fears in view of the uncertainties and contrary events of nature and life. Hume's treatment in this, as in most of his other works, has the decided merit of showing clearly where the true issue lies. If man's nature is not conceived of as spiritual, and religion is not regarded as springing from the depths of that nature in the consciousness of a relation to a supra-natural power, necessity is laid on the theorist of accounting for it from purely psychological, *i.e.*, *non*-religious and *ir*-rational, causes. This is precisely what Hume attempts to do in the treatise in question. His work is not only the precursor of that long train of "natural histories of religion" with which the "Science of Religion" has made us so familiar, but is wonderfully acute in some of its anticipations of modern theories. Dr. Tylor will readily recognise his "animistic" principle in such a sentence as the following: "There is a universal tendency among men to conceive all beings like themselves, and to transfer to every object those qualities of which they are intimately conscious."[3] Through

[1] Works, iv. p. 419. [2] *Ibid.* iv. p. 420. [3] *Ibid.* iv. p. 429.

this principle, with the help of the "allegorising" (as moderns would say, "mythological") tendency, and the deification of heroes, Hume believes himself able to explain the rise of polytheism—in his view the earliest form of religion, and the only one possible to man, when he was yet "a barbarous, necessitous animal."[1] The next step is to show how "this gross polytheism of the vulgar" passed into monotheism; and here Hume may certainly claim to be original. He explains the transition wholly by reference to the tendency in men to magnify and flatter those on whom they depend.[2] The same principle of flattery leads them to ascribe to the Deity the formation of the world. This is on a level with his theory of the origin of "priests," who, he says, "may justly be regarded as proceeding from one of the grossest inventions of a timorous and abject superstition."[3] He goes on, finally, to compare these two forms of religion —polytheism and monotheism—in their character and effects, the result in every case turning out in favour of polytheism. Thus, in regard to toleration: "The intolerance of almost all religions which have maintained the unity of God, is as remarkable as the contrary principle of polytheists."[4] Having thus completely nullified his

[1] Works, iv. p. 422. Hume's statements on this point are not, indeed, consistent. "It is a matter of fact incontestable," he says in one place, "that about 1700 years ago all mankind were polytheists" (p. 420); the Jews apparently count for nothing. But ere long we read: "The doctrine of one Supreme Deity, the author of nature, is very ancient; has spread over great and populous nations," etc. (p. 445). . . . "The Getes . . . were genuine theists and unitarians. They affirmed Zamolxis, their deity, to be the only true God," etc. (p. 452).

[2] Sec. 6.

[3] Works, iv. p. 79.

[4] Works, iv. p. 458. On this view, we must conclude, Rome did not persecute the Christians, missionaries have not been massacred by idolators, etc. Altogether, what is said of the tolerance of polytheists

original concession, he concludes with a few general corollaries, of which the satire is scarcely concealed.

But Hume has not left us in ignorance of the real value he put on the theistic proof—that "admirable adjustment of final causes"[1]—which on occasion we find him extolling. His posthumous *Dialogues concerning Natural Religion*, and his Essay on "Providence and a Future State," bear mainly on this and related topics. The *Dialogues*, elaborated and revised with the utmost care, and bequeathed to his executors under stringent provisions for their publication,[2] may be regarded as the most mature expression of his opinions on these grave subjects of any of his works. They are constructed somewhat on the model of Cicero's discussion on the Nature of the Gods, and close in language almost identical with his.[3] Hume evidently regards the whole question of Theism as a perfectly open one. As much can always be said on the one side as on the other; or rather, as he exerts himself in the sceptical interest to show, generally a great deal more against Theism than for it. Demea, the defender of a faith that repudiates reason, serves

has to be taken with considerable limitations. Rome had laws enough against foreign rites; even when they were permitted, the permission did not extend to Romans. Hume's own tender mercies towards "enthusiasts" in religion were not great. See below, p. 232.

[1] Works, iv. p. 431.

[2] See above, p. 83.

[3] "The conversation ended here and we parted. Velleius judged that the arguments of Cotta (the Academic) were truest; but those of Balbus (Stoic, and defender of the gods) seemed to me to have the greater probability" (Cicero).

"Cleanthes and Philo pursued not this conversation much further. . . . I confess that, upon a serious review of the whole, I cannot but think that Philo's arguments are more probable than Demea's; but that those of Cleanthes approached still nearer to the truth" (Hume).

mainly as a foil to the other two disputants; of the latter, it is easy to see that it is into the arguments of Philo, the sceptic, that Hume puts his whole strength; while Cleanthes, with his solemn rhetoric about the testimony which universal creation bears to "its intelligent Author" ("the whole chorus of nature raises one hymn to the praises of its Creator"),[1] advances arguments only to have the bottom taken out of them by Philo, and in any case does not argue for more than a being "finitely perfect, though far exceeding mankind."[2] It is Cleanthes with whom, as we saw, Hume would have his friends believe that he is personally most in agreement;[3] but as Philo does no more than reason from Hume's own principles on causation and the nature of mind, and in every case gains an easy argumentative victory over his opponent, it is difficult to credit this preference. If, towards the close, Philo himself is allowed to assume the pious rôle, and declaim on his "adoration to the Divine Being, as he discovers himself to reason, in the inexplicable contrivance and artifice of nature,"[4] one knows what value to put on this profession, while the previous reasonings are unrefuted. On both sides, of course, the disputants have a cultivated "abhorrence of vulgar superstitions."[5] How far Hume *did* allow any academic value to the theistic arguments is considered below.

The question of Theism, in a speculative point of view, is at bottom simply that of a rational and moral constitution in men and things. Man as a rational

[1] Works, ii. p. 458. [2] *Ibid.* ii. p. 507.

[3] See his correspondence with Elliot referred to above (Burton, i. pp. 331–2), and the close of the *Dialogues.*

[4] *Ibid.* ii. p. 552. [5] *Ibid.* ii. p. 529.

being, finds himself in a rationally-constituted universe; he cannot, therefore, without self-contradiction, construe it to himself otherwise than as proceeding from an intelligence kindred in principle with his own.[1] He is self-conscious and personal; he cannot, therefore, think of the ultimate principle and cause of things in terms *lower* than those of self-consciousness and personality. He is above all moral, and cannot, without renunciation of his ethical standpoint, regard the universe as other than a moral system, proceeding from a moral will, and subserving moral ends. The theist, in other words, takes in earnest, what Hume can at most admit only dialectically or sceptically, that Deity is "MIND OR THOUGHT,"[2] and draws out this admission to its legitimate conclusions. From this standpoint everything in religion assumes a new aspect, and admits of a new interpretation, from the dim gropings of the savage after a Higher than himself, whose presence he feels even where he cannot articulately express the nature of his feelings, to the tendency constantly evinced in thought and aspiration to rise from the finite to the infinite, from the caused to the uncaused, from the temporal to the eternal, from the conditioned to the unconditioned. To one occupying this standpoint, Hume's sceptical dialectics, based on the contrary assumption of the *non*-rational constitution of man and of the universe, must always appear frivolous.

What are his objections to the theistic hypothesis?

[1] Cf. T. H. Green, *Prol. to Ethics*, p. 23: "The understanding which presents an order of nature to us is in principle one with an understanding which constitutes that order itself."

[2] Works, ii. p. 526.

First, and perhaps mainly, that the whole subject is "quite beyond the reach of our faculties."[1] The analogy between what we call thought in man and the infinite intelligence we assume as the cause of the universe, is so inconceivably remote, that no inference from one to the other is warrantable.

"What peculiar advantage has this little agitation of the brain which we call *thought*, that we must thus make it the model of the whole universe? . . . If thought, as we may well suppose, be confined merely to this narrow corner, and has even there so limited a sphere of action, with what propriety can we assign it for the cause of all things?"[2]

In the next place, our belief in causation rests solely on the *custom* of seeing objects and events in invariable conjunction,[3] and therefore fails us where, as in the present case, custom cannot operate. "Our ideas reach no further than experience," but "we have no experience of divine attributes and operations."[4] In causation we are entitled only to infer from observed cases to similar cases; but here, "does not the great disproportion bar all comparison and inference?"[5] Reasoning from causation rests on *experienced* conjunctions; but there is no "experience of the origin of worlds." How can the argument have place "where the objects, as in the present case, are singular, individual, without parallel or specific resemblance"?[6] As he puts the point in the Essay on Providence, the world is "a singular effect."[7] Or, viewing the cause as an ideal plan in the divine mind, must we not say that

[1] Works, ii. pp. 421, 431.
[2] *Ibid.* ii. pp. 438–9.
[3] *Ibid.* ii. p. 441.
[4] *Ibid.* ii. pp. 431, 438.
[5] *Ibid.* ii. p. 438.
[6] *Ibid.* ii. p. 441.
[7] *Ibid.* ii. p. 168.

this collocation of ideas needs another cause to explain *it*, and so *ad infinitum*. Hume's reasoning here is so deliciously illustrative of the conception he forms of a rational mind, that a few sentences must be quoted:—

"Have we not the same reason to trace that ideal world into another ideal world, or new intelligent principle? But if we stop, and go no further; why go so far? Why not stop at the material world? . . . To say that the different ideas which compose the reason of the Supreme Being, fall into order of themselves, and by their own nature, is really to talk without meaning. If it has a meaning, I would fain know, why it is not as good sense to say, that the parts of the material world fall into order of themselves, and by their own nature. . . . If it requires a cause in both, what do we gain by your system in tracing the universe of objects into a similar universe of ideas? The first step which we make leads us on for ever. It were therefore wise in us to limit all our inquiries to the present world, without looking further."[1]

The whole point being, that a rational mind *can* think, and form a plan, while the parts of the material world cannot.

A more trenchant, because really inductive, argument is based on the imperfection, evil, and misery of the world, which, it is argued, negatives the idea of a perfectly wise and beneficent author of the universe.[2] Mr. Mill's famous indictment of Nature in his *Three Essays on Religion*[3] is ably anticipated in these sec-

[1] Works, ii. pp. 455–6. Cf. on the *modus operandi* of thinking—"The ideas in a human mind, we see, by an unknown, inexplicable economy, arrange themselves so as to form the plan of a watch or house" (p. 436).

[2] Parts X., XI.

[3] Pp. 28 ff.

tions of Hume's. In the Essay on Providence and a Future State the argument is directed to prove that the safety of the State and social order generally are as secure without the belief in a providence as with it. For, Hume reasons, on the principle that we are not entitled to put into the cause more than we find in the effect, it is illegitimate to ascribe to the Creator greater perfection than already belongs to the material order, taken by itself. The order of the world being in any case what it is, the assumption of a providence adds nothing to it, and the argument for a future life based on the injustices of the present state likewise falls. For we have no warrant to infer any more perfect justice than the facts of the present disclose. To Hume's reasoning, like Mill's, it must be replied, first, that their picture of the evil and misery wrought by mere nature is egregiously overcharged. On Hume's principles, the only consistent philosophy of existence would be Pessimism. But the description is an exaggeration. The "nature red in tooth and claw" theory is only one aspect of the facts. There is sound sense in Paley's rejoinder: "It is a happy world after all. The air, the earth, the waters teem with delighted existence."[1] But next, it is not solely on induction from nature that belief in the perfection of the Creator is established. It stands or falls, in truth, with the reality of the moral ideal. The man whose faith is anchored there will not lack the power to discern a moral system, if in imperfect degree, even in nature.

How then has the universe, with its wondrous "adjustments," which are not denied, come into exist-

[1] *Nat. Theol.*, ch. xxvi. Cf. Dr. H. Stirling's *Darwinism*, pp. 205 ff.

ence? That problem remains, even if the theistic explanation is rejected. Here, in the person of his sceptic, Hume fairly revels in hypotheses. It would hardly seem as if there need be any difficulty—so fertile is he in the invention of theories. Need there be any cause at all? For the principle of causation, engendered through custom, has no application beyond the sphere of experience. Or why should not the world, as the old philosophers thought, be analogous to an animal or vegetable, having the principle of its development within itself?[1] Order, arrangement, or the adjustment of final causes, is not of itself any proof of design; "but only so far as it has been experienced to proceed from that principle."[2] Nay, even the Epicurean hypothesis of a "fortuitous concourse of atoms" is not beyond defence:—

"A finite number of particles is only susceptible of finite transpositions; and it must happen, in an eternal duration, that every possible order or position must be tried an infinite number of times. . . . No one, who has a conception of the powers of infinite, in comparison of finite, will ever scruple this determination."[3]

It would be idle to refute these phantasies. The fallacy of the last lies in supposing that the fortuitous clashing of elements even through infinite duration must result in all possible combinations—even such as we attribute to mind. *That*, it is certain, an aimless concourse would never do; any more than compositor's types clashing together to all eternity would produce an *Iliad*, a *Hamlet*, or a *Treatise of Human Nature*, though that is a possible combination of them. The matter is not mended when, as in Darwinism, processes

[1] Works, ii. p. 468. [2] *Ibid.* ii. p. 436. [3] *Ibid.* ii. p. 481.

essentially fortuitous are clothed with sounding titles like "natural selection" and "survival of the fittest."

In the Essay on the Immortality of the Soul, suppressed in Hume's lifetime,[1] similar modes of reasoning are employed to destroy all physical or metaphysical arguments for immortality. It seems to Hume that, in words already quoted, "if any purpose of nature be clear, we may affirm that the whole scope and intention of man's creation, so far as we can judge by natural reason, is limited to the present life."[2] Widely different has been the judgment formed of man's capacities by other and deeper thinkers, from Plato down to Wordsworth and Browning, and even J. S. Mill![3] The Essay commences and concludes in Hume's most reprehensible mock-pious style:—

"In reality it is the gospel, and the gospel alone, which has brought life and immortality to light."[4]

"Nothing could set in a fuller light the infinite obligations which mankind have to divine revelation, since we find that no other medium could ascertain this great and important truth."[5]

A "truth," which is represented in the Essay not only as unsupported by reason, but as positively outraging it!

Is Hume's final attitude to Theism, then, to be described as one of absolute negation, or only as one of scepticism? If regard be had solely to the principles of his philosophy, there can be no hesitation as to the answer; for through them the foundations of Theism are undeniably destroyed. On the other hand, if any

[1] See above, p. 58. [2] Works, iv. p. 549.
[3] Cf. Mill's striking remarks in his *Three Essays*, pp. 249–50.
[4] *Ibid.* iv. p. 547. [5] *Ibid.* iv. p. 555.

weight is to be attached to Hume's own repeated professions,—if they are not simply to be regarded as accommodations to popular opinion, like his admiration for "our most holy religion,"—he did stop short in practice of this extreme position, and gave Theism the benefit of the Academic doubt. The frame of things, he would allow, *did* suggest the idea of an intelligent author, though the instant the solvents of reason were applied to it, the grounds of that belief, or tendency to belief, vanished.[1] But when the utmost is granted to Hume that he ever thought of claiming, his Theism is found to be a purely speculative, inoperative thing, hardly deserving to be described by so dignified a name. It is a Theism between which and atheism, as comes out in the close of the *Dialogues*,[2] the difference is only verbal. It amounts to no more than the acknowledgment of the probability "that the principle which first arranged, and still maintains order in the universe," bears also "some remote inconceivable analogy to the other operations of nature, and among the rest, to the economy of human nature and thought."[3] In respect of moral attributes—if such can be spoken of at all—this "principle" is at a still greater remove from man.[4] Moreover, this belief in Deity, such as it is, is entirely otiose. It is not allowed, any more than the idle belief of the Epicurean in his gods, to have any influence on affection or conduct. It excludes prayer. As Hume succinctly summed it up in his letter on Dr. Leechman's sermon, the religion of the rational

[1] Huxley observes: "Hume's theism, such as it is, dissolves away in the dialectic river, until nothing is left but the verbal sack in which it was contained" (*Hume*, p. 146).

[2] Works, ii. pp. 527–8. [3] *Ibid.* ii. p. 528. [4] *Ibid.*; cf. p. 502.

man is confined to "the practice of morality, and the assent of the understanding to the proposition *that God exists*."[1] Here Hume drew the line for himself, with a large mark of interrogation behind.

Hume's task, however, was not yet finished. On the basis of reasonings like the above, the fate of historical revelation was no longer doubtful. Since, however, in that age, belief in revelation was supposed to be supported chiefly by the evidence of miracles, it remained for Hume, as the culmination of his philosophical undertaking, to subvert effectually that reputed foundation of the Christian religion. This is the work he takes in hand in the most famous of all his sceptical writings—the Essay on Miracles. It has been seen in an earlier chapter how the idea of the Essay originated.[2] Hume himself, with that complacency which never failed him when judging of his own performances, regarded its reasonings as absolutely fatal to the belief assailed.

"I flatter myself," he says, "that I have discovered an argument of like nature [to that of Tillotson against transubstantiation], which, if just, will, with the wise and learned, be an everlasting check to all kinds of superstitious delusion, and consequently will be useful as long as the world endures; for so long, I presume, will the accounts of miracles and prodigies be found in all history, sacred and profane."[3]

[1] Burton, i. p. 162. See above, p. 37. [2] See above, p. 26.

[3] Works, iv. p. 125. Hume's argument was reviewed by La Place, the French astronomer, in his *Sur les Probabilities*, and was supported by an elaborate criticism in the *Edinburgh Review* (No. 46), universally attributed to Professor Leslie. The most noted of the many replies was that of Dr. Campbell of Aberdeen. His *Dissertation on Miracles* (see above, p. 61) is an acute and well-reasoned production.

Notwithstanding this preliminary flourish of trumpets, it is not difficult to show that this celebrated argument of Hume's, *in the form in which he presents it*, is little better than an elaborate sophism. Its essence may be said to be contained in the two following propositions:—

"A miracle is a violation of the laws of nature, and as a firm and unalterable experience has established these laws, the proof against a miracle, from the nature of the case, is as entire as any argument from experience can possibly be imagined."[1]

"No testimony is sufficient to establish a miracle unless this testimony be of such a kind that its falsehood would be more miraculous than the fact which it endeavours to establish."[2]

Something might be said *in limine* on the definition of a miracle as a "violation" of the laws of nature, and on the manifest inconsistency of the reasoning with Hume's own account of the origin of our belief in the uniformity of nature. How can a belief which is simply a product of custom—of subjective association of our ideas—be set up as a bar against any number of "violations" of the ordinary course of nature? To make good his contention, Hume would have to show that the power of custom was so strong that what he calls a "violation" of the laws of nature was not even *conceivable*, or at least *believable*, by us. But then his argument would not have been needed, and would have been stultified by his own admission that "accounts of miracles and prodigies" are found in all history.[3]

[1] Works, iv. p. 130. [2] *Ibid.* iv. p. 131.

[3] Part of Hume's argument against Theism in the *Dialogues* is that Deity might have prevented the evils flowing from "general laws" by means of "particular volitions" (Works, ii. p. 511).

More important is the objection that, taken on its own merits, the argument is a glaring begging of the question. "A firm and unalterable experience," Hume says, "has established these laws." Even this, it may be remarked in passing, is an erroneous statement. Belief in a law of nature does not, as a rule, rest on any such induction from universal experience. How, if it did, could the "firm and unalterable experience" ever be proved? Many laws are quite recent discoveries, and rest on a very few observed instances. A few crucial experiments in a laboratory may establish the existence of a law to the satisfaction of all thinking men. Besides, as has often been pointed out, in this way of putting it, there can be no proper contrast between "experience" and "testimony," or room for the mathematical weighing of the one against the other. All the experience we have on this or any similar point, except our own, *is* testimony—only reaches us through testimony.

Two things may be supposed to be covered by Hume's statement that "a firm and unalterable experience has established" the laws of nature. It may mean (1) that experience has established *that there are laws of nature;* or (2) that experience has established *that no events ever take place in "violation" of these laws.* On either supposition the reasoning must be pronounced fallacious. No one questions that there are laws of nature; the strength of the argument must lie, therefore, in the assertion that "firm and unalterable experience" has established that none but natural causes have ever been concerned in the production of events—that natural laws, in Hume's phrase, have never been "violated." But this is very manifestly the begging of the very point at issue. For the assertion of a miracle is precisely the assertion that this has *not* been the universal experience. The "firm and unalterable experience" can only be gained by discrediting beforehand all testimony to miracle; by refusing it a hearing. "It is a miracle," Hume says, "that a dead man should ever come to life, because that has never been observed in any age or country."[1] But then, has it not? That is the very question to be answered. There is no need for going through the form of an argument, if the whole matter is to be taken for granted at the outset. Better say at once with Mr. Arnold—"Miracles do not happen"[2]—and leave it so.

Mr. J. S. Mill is conscious of this weakness of Hume's argument, and seeks to avoid some of these objections by giving it a new turn. He interprets it to mean simply that no testimony can ever prevail against a complete induction.[3] This is not the shape that Hume himself gave it; but even so, it is interesting to observe that Mr. Mill does not admit its cogency. The assertion of a miracle, he concedes, contradicts nothing which the experience of mankind has "firmly and unalterably established." His own words are worth quoting. "In order that any alleged fact," he says, "should be contradictory to a law of causation, the allegation must be, not simply that the cause existed without being followed by the effect, for that would be no uncommon occurrence; but that this happened in the absence of any adequate counteracting cause. Now, in the case of an alleged miracle, the assertion is the exact opposite of this. It is, that

[1] Works, iv. p. 130. [2] Preface to *Literature and Dogma* (1883).
[3] *Logic*, ii. p. 151.

the effect was defeated, not in the absence, but in consequence of a counteracting cause, namely, a direct interposition of an act of the will of some being who has power over nature; and in particular of a Being, whose will being assumed to have endowed all the causes with the powers by which they produce their effects, may well be supposed able to counteract them. . . . Of the adequacy of that cause, if present, there can be no doubt; and the only antecedent improbability which can be ascribed to the miracle is the improbability that any such cause existed."[1]

What real cogency Hume's argument possesses does not lie in these logical subtleties, based on an assumed "firm and unalterable experience," but in the other direction of the strong antecedent improbability of deviations from the known course of nature, as compared with the admitted fallibility of human testimony. Every one recognises that the presumption against a really miraculous event is so strong as, in ordinary circumstances, to be practically insuperable. As Hume argues, the course of nature is uniform, while human testimony is notoriously fallible. How, then, shall the one ever be successfully pitted against the other? The simply *unusual* is frequently discredited on this ground, often with an excess of scepticism;[2] how much more the positively *miraculous?* Even here, however, it may be shown that Hume

[1] *Logic*, pp. 161–2. Cf. Brown in *Cause and Effect* (notes A and F): "A miracle is no contradiction of the law of cause and effect; it is a new effect supposed to be produced by the introduction of a new cause."

[2] Cf. Hume's case of the Indian prince (from Locke) refusing to believe in water freezing because he had never seen it (Works, iv. p. 129).

pushes his argument beyond its due bounds. The improbability in question is felt when the circumstances are ordinary; but what if they are *extraordinary?* Hume assumes that the presumption against a miracle must always be practically infinite. But everything here depends on circumstances. It is quite conceivable that the circumstances may be such as not only to create no antecedent presumption against the miracle, but to yield a strong presumption for it. A miracle, that is, can never be treated as a wholly isolated event. If it is, the presumption against it will be invariably strong. If the miracle, in addition to being sporadic, is frivolous or absurd, as, *e.g.*, in the case of Mr. Arnold's prodigy of the pen being turned into a pen-wiper,[1] or Professor Huxley's centaur trotting down the street,[2] it may be summarily dismissed from consideration. Where, on the other hand, the miracle is not isolated, but stands in a context which renders it rational and credible, the case is widely altered. Given, *e.g.*,—to state the Christian position—such a Person as Jesus Christ declared Himself to be, the miracles that are attributed to Him become in the highest degree *natural*—events to be expected from such an One. Given, again, a great scheme of divine revelation, extending through many ages, in successive historical dispensations, it is in itself anything but incredible that miracles should have been employed in the founding of these dispensations, or in connection with them. Even in nature, it can be argued, the founding of a new kingdom, or rise from a lower to a higher—as at the introduction of life—cannot well be construed without something analogous

[1] *Lit. and Dogma*, p. 95 (1883). [2] *Hume*, p. 134.

to miracle. This is a class of considerations of which Hume takes no account—perhaps was incapable of appreciating.

But Hume shows himself equally in error in unduly belittling the force of the testimony for miracle. Here, as in the other case, everything depends on circumstances. Human testimony may generally be very faulty; but there are instances in which testimony is given by such persons, of such character, and under such conditions, that it would do more violence to reason wholly to reject, than it would do to accept, their witness. Testimony is not to be measured by the mathematical rules of which Hume is so fond—so many instances for the general rule, so many for this particular exception to it. There is not necessarily any real contradiction between the two sets of experiences. Contradiction can only arise where, of two persons on the spot, one affirms and the other denies. When the two conditions which have been mentioned coincide: (1) a presumption in the nature of the case, not against, but for the miracle; and (2) the testimony of reliable witnesses, in cases where the matter is one on which they are plainly competent to judge, the evidence for miracle, instead of being weak, may be very strong indeed.[1]

It may be noted as a last criticism on Hume's argument, that it narrows down the testimony for miracles too exclusively to *individual* testimony. It is over-

[1] On the parallels which Hume draws in his Essay between the miracles at the tomb of the Abbé de Paris and the Christian miracles, the reader had better suspend his judgment till he has studied the real facts about the former, as brought out by Campbell, Leland, and others, in their respective replies to Hume.

looked that miracle may be verifiable on the *large* scale as well as on the *small*, so that it may sometimes be easier to establish the supernatural character of a general system, than to verify all the particular miracles connected with it as parts or corollaries. Even as respects testimony, the individual form is far from being the only, or always, even, the most important one. There is, *e.g.*, such a thing as the testimony of the *collective* or *national* consciousness, which may retain the memory of great events, where individual witnesses can no longer be identified; or, as in Christianity, the witness of the consciousness of the historic *Church* to the great facts connected with its origin. But this class of considerations, again, is quite foreign to the mode of thought of our author, who, confident of having destroyed the defences of revealed religion, closes with great satisfaction in his usual strain of satire:—

"So that, upon the whole, we may conclude that the *Christian Religion* not only was at first attended with miracles, but even at this day cannot be believed by any reasonable person without one. Mere reason is insufficient to convince us of its veracity; and whoever is moved by *Faith* to assent to it is conscious of a continued miracle in his own person, which subverts all the principles of his understanding, and gives him a determination to believe what is most contrary to custom and experience."[1]

[1] Works, iv. p. 150.

CHAPTER XI

HUME'S MISCELLANEOUS WRITINGS: POLITICAL ECONOMY—HUME AS HISTORIAN

UNDER the heading of "Miscellaneous Writings," we have in view chiefly the *Essays Moral and Political*, originally published in 1741–2 (changes and additions after), and the *Political Discourses*, which appeared first in 1752—the whole subsequently comprised under *Essays and Treatises on several Subjects.*[1] The *Essays* were Hume's first popular writings, and in the main deserved their popularity. They are written with excellent taste and finish, and, though by no means the most important part of Hume's contribution to literature, are nearly always learned, thoughtful, and suggestive. As already told, they were commenced with a view to weekly publication on the model of the *Spectator* and the *Craftsman*,[2] and affect the easy, natural treatment proper to that class of composition. Dividing the "elegant part of mankind" into "the learned and the conversible," Hume describes himself as a "kind of ambassador" whose mission it is to promote a good correspondence between the two States.[3] He accepts Addison's definition of fine writing as con-

[1] On the history of the Editions, see Appendix.

[2] See above, p. 36.

[3] "Of Essay Writing," Works, iv. p. 519.

sisting of sentiments which are natural, without being obvious;[1] and sets it before him as his aim to earn that distinction for his own performances. Save, however, for some papers of the slighter sort, afterwards dropped, the *Essays* are of too solid and durable a quality to be well adapted for the purposes of mere "polite" recreation. Even the abstrusest of them is marked by the utmost literary care. No one who reads the papers on "Delicacy of Taste," on "Eloquence," on "Simplicity and Refinement in Writing," will doubt that Hume had bestowed great pains on the study of style, and on the canons of literary excellence generally, and that, however curiously awry some of his own critical judgments unquestionably were, he entertained on the whole very correct views on these subjects. The Essay on "The Standard of Taste," in particular (later in date than the others), is in its way a model of fine writing on a purely literary theme. It abounds in just and discriminating observations, and manifests on every page the author's own refinement of judgment and delicacy of taste. A favourite method of Hume in the *Essays* is to lay down his thesis in the form of a paradox, bringing up first all that can be said against it, then proceeding to explain, illustrate, and defend his own position.

One incidental advantage of the *Essays* is that they frequently afford interesting side-lights on Hume's opinions in regard to subjects other than those of which the Essay directly treats. The "abstruse philosophy" is now, indeed, left wholly behind. "Impressions and ideas" have disappeared, and we stand on the broad ground of common humanity. The trans-

[1] "Of Simplicity and Refinement," Works, iii. p. 211.

formation is so curious that the reflective reader can hardly help sometimes being amused by it. No longer are causes and effects arbitrary conjunctions of phenomena, but "effects will always correspond to causes,"[1] and the rational connection between the two is so clearly seen, that effect may be deduced from cause with perfect certainty. The principles from which the author reasons are no longer precarious subjective assumptions, but "eternal and immutable truths." E.g.:—

"So great is the force of laws, and of particular forms of government, and so little dependence have they on the humours and tempers of men, that consequences almost as general and certain may sometimes be deduced from them as anything which the mathematical sciences afford us."

The "inconveniences" of an elective monarchy are "such as are founded on causes and principles eternal and immutable."

"An observation of Machiavel . . . which, I think, may be regarded as one of those eternal political truths which no time nor accidents can vary."[2]

A special interest attaches to the "political" *Essays*, as showing how Hume's mind, even at this early date, was working forward to his great *History*. Most of the principles of the *History*, in fact, are already here *in nuce*. There is already the evidence of extensive reading in the history of the past, of keen powers of observation, of accurate comparison of forms of political government, of the habit of mind that is not content till it has traced effects to their causes, and particular facts to the general principles that explain them.

[1] Works, iii. p. 20.

[2] On "Politics a Science," Works, iii. pp. 12, 14, 18.

There is the same wide knowledge of human nature, and interest in its workings, as in the *History;* the same philosophic impartiality, or affectation of it; the same inability to comprehend the profounder springs of human action; the same intense antipathy to "priesthood" and "fanaticism." In one of his letters he says of the Essay on the Protestant Succession: "I treat that subject as coolly and indifferently as I would the dispute between Cæsar and Pompey."[1] His views on the general principles of government, and the workings of different constitutions, are based on a wide induction from Greek and Roman, Venetian, Italian, French, and other forms of rule, and are frequently marked by shrewd insight. His own judgment is in favour of such a balance of the constitution as existed in England—a "mixed monarchy," with a hereditary ruler—though from the first there is all too favourable an estimate of the effects of despotism.

"It may, therefore, be pronounced," he says, "as an universal axiom in politics, *That an hereditary prince, a nobility without vassals, and a people voting by their representatives, form the best* MONARCHY, ARISTOCRACY, and DEMOCRACY."[2] Yet, while not unfriendly to a republic in the abstract, he avows:—

"I would frankly declare that, though liberty be preferable to slavery, in almost every case, yet I should rather wish to see an absolute monarch than a republic in this Island."[3]

One thing which unduly biassed Hume in favour of absolutism was what he took to be the peculiar success of that form of monarchy in France.[4] Though not blind

[1] Burton, i. p. 239.
[2] Works, iii. p. 15.
[3] *Ibid.* iii. p. 52.
[4] *Ibid.* iii. pp. 98, 102.

to the evils of oppressive taxation in that country, he had not the dimmest perception of the terrible catastrophe that was preparing beneath the brilliant surface he beheld, and thought the mischiefs could be remedied by a better system of finance.[1] He was strangely insensible to the evils of even such a government as that of Turkey, and had a high opinion of the "integrity, gravity, and bravery" of the Turkish people; "a candid, sincere people," he calls them.[2]

Yet there is a difference between the earlier and the later Hume on this point of attachment to political liberty, though it must be owned that the distinction is at best a relative one. When Hume first wrote, the English Revolution was not far behind, and the Crown had long been dependent on Whig support. But change was impending, and, while Hume's sympathies were in the main with freedom, he took up, from his philosophic standpoint, a very detached attitude to parties in general. He says of his Essay on the Protestant Succession, "The conclusion shows me a Whig, but a very sceptical one."[3] Walpole, the head of the party, had been in power for well-nigh a generation, and, in an Essay which he wrote on that statesman, (afterwards reduced to a note), Hume showed that he had formed by no means too flattering a judgment on his character and administration. "During his time," he says, "trade has flourished, liberty declined, and learning gone to ruin. As I am a man, I love him; as I am a scholar, I hate him; as I am a Briton, I calmly wish his fall."[4] Probably the most genuine evidence of his interest in freedom is his defence (still how far

[1] Works, iii. p. 103.
[2] *Ibid.* iii. pp. 225, 232.
[3] Burton, i. p. 239.
[4] Works, iii. p. 27.

from the elevated note of Milton!) of the liberty of the press in his Essay on that subject in the earlier editions. In the course of the discussion he says:—

"It has also been proved, as the experience of mankind increases, that the people are no such dangerous monsters as they have been represented, and that it is in every respect better to guide them like rational creatures than to lead or drive them like brute beasts."[1]

But it is significant that the passages containing these liberal sentiments were subsequently expunged; and at the close of his Essay on Parties in Great Britain he made a yet more general retractation. "Some of the opinions in these *Essays,*" he writes, "with regard to the public transactions in the last century, the author, on more accurate examination, found occasion to retract in his *History of Great Britain*. . . . Nor is he ashamed to acknowledge his mistakes. These mistakes were, indeed, at that time, almost universal in that kingdom."[2]

Of all Hume's Essays, however, the most important are unquestionably those originally published under the title of *Political Discourses.* In the present state of economical science, indeed, the Essays contain scarcely anything which we may not find much better stated elsewhere; but in a historical respect, they form a link in the development of that science of no mean importance. "The Political Discourses of Mr. Hume," says Dugald Stewart, in his life of Adam Smith, "were certainly of greater use to Mr. Smith than any other book that had appeared prior to his Lectures." Adam Smith, strangely enough, does not take much direct notice of Hume in the *Wealth of Nations*, but the

[1] Works, iii. p. 10. [2] *Ibid.* iii. p. 76.

careful reader will easily discern Hume's influence, and will observe that, incidentally, there are few of Hume's speculations which are not taken up, and carefully considered. In this connection, the Essays on "Money," "Interest," "The Balance of Trade," "The Jealousy of Trade," "Taxes," and "Public Credit," are the most important. The spirit in all these papers is identical with that of the *Wealth of Nations*. In the very first sentence of the Essay on Money, *e.g.*, we have the key-note of Smith's epoch-making work:—

"Money is not, properly speaking, one of the subjects of commerce. . . . It is indeed evident that money is nothing but the representation of labour and commodities, and serves only as a means of rating or estimating them."[1]

Hence the folly, Hume goes on to show, of supposing, as had been done by nearly all European nations, that the real wealth of a country could be increased by the mere increase of its gold and silver. This is exactly the error which, under the name of "The Mercantile System," Adam Smith spends his strength in combating, sometimes in language that might seem almost an echo of Hume's own. On certain minor points, indeed, he differs from Hume; for instance, on the question whether, even in the case of war, or of any negotiations with a foreign power, an abundance of the precious metals is, as Hume supposes, any real advantage. But in regard to main principles, the two are perfectly at one. So, again, on the question of Commerce and Free Trade, Hume shows unanswerably, as Smith did more fully after him, that no policy can ever be wholesome which attempts to place restraints either on

[1] Works, iii. p. 309.

home manufacture or on foreign commerce. He maintains the thesis that the tendency of industry, arts, and trades is to increase the power of the sovereign, as well as the happiness of the subject. The true policy of any country, therefore, must ever be to encourage trade and manufacture, as bringing commodities into the market, and into contact with the circulating *specie.* As in the former case, there are parts of Hume's exposition to which well-grounded exception may be taken; but, on the whole, his defence of the principle of unrestricted competition will bear comparison with that of his more illustrious successor. It is strange that with such clear views of the fallacies involved in the idea of a "Balance of Trade," Hume should have remained so enamoured as he was of the idea of a "Balance of Power" in politics. He regarded this as "a secret in politics fully known only to the present age,"[1] and devoted an Essay to the discussion of the question, "Whether the idea of the balance of power be owing entirely to modern policy, or whether the phrase only has been invented in these later ages."[2] He was not, withal, insensible to the fact that the principle had been pushed much too far in the politics of his time.[3] In certain other respects, as in his idea that a tax on German linen "encourages home manufactures and thereby multiplies our people and industry," and that a tax on brandy "increases the sale of rum, and supports our foreign colonies,"[4] he is clearly in inconsistency with his own principles. It is chiefly, however, on the subject of bank credit, paper-currency, and related topics, that his views, though ingeniously

[1] Works, iii. p. 100.
[2] *Ibid.* iii. p. 364.
[3] *Ibid.* iii. p. 371.
[4] *Ibid.* iii. p. 356.

explained and defended, are out of accord with those of modern economists, and have been most convincingly refuted by experience.[1] Hume was unduly influenced by the dread of "banishing" the precious metals from the country; a fear from which, again, his own reasonings might have saved him. But he confesses that the subject is "extremely complicated," and states fairly enough the advantages of the system he opposes.[2]

The originality of the economical speculations of Hume will hardly be questioned. He had few predecessors in England,[3] and the French economists, Quesnay, Turgot, and others of their school, had not yet written. In fact, a powerful influence of Hume may be traced in these authors, as well as in Adam Smith.[4] The *Discourses* were early translated into French, and Turgot himself produced a translation of several of them.

It remains now to speak of Hume in that department of his work in which his fame culminated, viz., as historian.

A truly great History is a work of art. Lord Macaulay represents history as occupying the border land between reason and imagination, and therefore as coming partly under the jurisdiction of both. The solid qualities of the historian—learning, veracity, sound sense—are all important; but he fails in the higher department of his work if he cannot, in addition, throw over the details of his narration the fresh interest and warm glow of imagination; if he cannot

[1] Works, iii. pp. 311, 347 ff. [2] *Ibid.* iii. p. 349.

[3] Dugald Stewart has a note on some of these in his *Life of Adam Smith.*

[4] Cf. Burton, i. p. 365, and Dugald Stewart's *Life of Adam Smith.*

combine vivid and picturesque description of situations and incidents, with the philosophical exhibition of the course and connection of events. It was in these higher qualities of historical presentation that Hume showed himself a master. His *History*, as we shall immediately see, was far from perfect; abounded indeed in faults. But its excellences were also conspicuous. Gibbon declared that its ease and grace filled him "with a mixed sensation of delight and despair."[1] Hume has the rare art of presenting the circumstances of a long and complicated train of events in such a light that the art is hidden by the apparent naturalness of the arrangement. Few have excelled him in the picturesque and vivid grouping of details, and in the combination of elaborate description with clearness, simplicity, and ease. He has the eye of the artist for the things that contribute to dramatic effect; and when he finds a subject suited to his pen, as, for instance, the Gunpowder Conspiracy, or the meeting of the Long Parliament, or the trial of King Charles, or, on another plane, such a chapter of court scandal as the rise and amours of Somerset, he extends his canvas, and lingers to produce a picture which shall at once fill the mind and captivate the imagination. As in his other writings, so here, he makes skilful use of the principle of contrast; in a complex case, *e.g.*, setting forth first the reasons of one side, then those of the other, and finally summing up as the impartial spectator.[2] Beyond all, the *History* is characterised by the presence of a subtle yet unobtrusive vein of reflection,

[1] *Autobiography.*

[2] As examples, the chapters on the Gunpowder Plot and on the Petition of Rights may be compared.

which makes it in many parts a model of what "reflective" history ought to be. Hume's temper, commonly, is so even, his judgment so calm, in all matters where his own prejudices are not involved (unfortunately a serious qualification), that it would be a misfortune if, with all its faults, his *History* should ever be allowed to be forgotten. It was the first really great *History* of which our language could boast, and there are critics who doubt whether, in certain respects, it is not the best still.

The faults of the work, however, are equally manifest. They are such faults as were inevitable in any *History* proceeding from the mind of Hume. One must try, of course, to be scrupulously just to the author even here. If Hume took the side of arbitrary power to an extent which jars upon our sense of justice and impartiality, it may be allowed that he did so, not because he sympathised with tyranny as such, but because, in the circumstances, that seemed to him the side of order. His natural dislike of all turbulence and fanaticism operated strongly to prejudice him against the popular party in the nation, as well as against the principles with which that party was identified. A popular cause can never be altogether separated from inflamed passions, unreasonable excesses, extravagant demands, and misguided zeal. These abuses a calm and enlightened historian ought to have been able to distinguish from the true merits of the case. But Hume looked mainly to the faults. His high appreciation of the interests of learning and literature threw a powerful weight into the scale of the party possessed of the greatest education, politeness, and refinement. Still, after every allowance for the colour which must be given to every historian's narrative by the peculiar lights of his own mind, it is impossible to acquit Hume of making an unfair and careless use of his materials. Hallam, the model of a temperate and impartial historian, is compelled at times to speak in the strongest terms of his unreliability. Macaulay is himself far from blameless in the matter of bias, but his estimate of Hume can scarcely be accused of exaggeration. "Hume," he says, "is an accomplished advocate. Without positively asserting much more than he can prove, he gives prominence to all the circumstances which support his case; he glides lightly over those which are unfavourable to it; his own witnesses are applauded and encouraged; the statements which seem to throw discredit on them are contradicted; the contradictions into which they fall are explained away; a clear and connected abstract of their evidence is given. Everything that is offered on the other side is scrutinised with the utmost severity; every suspicious circumstance is a ground for comment and invective; what cannot be denied or extenuated is passed by without notice; concessions even are sometimes made; but the insidious candour only increases the effect of the vast mass of sophistry."[1]

The *History* was conceived and written, as Hume himself indicates, with a very definite purpose, viz., to correct what he supposed to be the "misrepresentations of factions" in connection with the reigns of the Stuarts.[2] Mr. Maurice has, we think, not unjustly connected this design of Hume's with the spirit of the so-called "Philosophical History" at that time in vogue

[1] On History, *Mis. Writings*, p. 154.

[2] *My Own Life.*

in France under the auspices of Voltaire.[1] History was to be made a popular and interesting medium for diffusing the principles of that "easy and obvious" philosophy, of which the essence was the absence of every high and ideal aim. The past was to be made to speak, as far as possible, the thoughts, the feelings, the temper of the present. Everything that might interfere with that temper—the belief in God, in providence, in eternal destiny—was to be skilfully extracted, and in this way the reader was to be trained to regard every attempt to rise above the sphere with which he was habitually conversant, as extravagant and ridiculous. Hume need not, indeed, be supposed to have formed any deliberate design of introducing these French modes of thought and literature into Scotland. It is asserted only that his *History* is strongly imbued with the same spirit and tendency. His mind was naturally disposed in this direction; the contagion was in the air, and he naturally caught the prevailing distemper.

The *History*, we saw,[2] was commenced in 1752, after Hume had been appointed Librarian to the Faculty of Advocates in Edinburgh. The influences already noticed had not a little to do with his choice of the accession of the House of Stuart as the starting-point of his undertaking. Then commenced in Britain, not merely the grand struggle between court and country, but also what Maurice calls "the great theocratical conflict" for religious principle and liberty of conscience. The fullest admission may be made of the grave faults, the uncultured narrowness, the manifestations of bigotry, which may frequently be charged

[1] *Mod. Phil.*, ch. ix.

[2] See above, pp. 50 ff.

against both English Puritans and Scotch Covenanters, though it is easily possible here to exaggerate. But what is inexcusable is that one should be indifferent to the higher meaning of these struggles, out of which have sprung nearly all our modern civil and religious rights and privileges. Hume himself, in a passage which is retained to the last edition, remarks on the Puritans, most inconsistently, indeed, with other parts of his work: "The precious spark of liberty had been kindled, and was preserved by the Puritans alone; it was to this sect, whose principles appear so frivolous, and their habits so ridiculous, that the English owe the whole freedom of their constitution."[1] If this was so, what is to be said of the historian who, in the same and in earlier volumes, condemns all, or nearly all, their important acts in the struggle for freedom, and as warmly espouses the cause of their opponents? For this is what Hume did. Throughout he was a zealous defender of the royal prerogative against the party identified with religion and constitutional liberty. Whatever evils may be supposed to attend an absolute monarchy, and he does not pretend to ignore them, they are not, in his judgment, comparable to the far worse evils which spring from anarchy and faction. And the chief source of anarchy and faction, in Hume's view, was religion, or, as he prefers to name it, "enthusiasm." The spirit of English freedom he believed to be inseparably associated in its progress with religious fanaticism and bigotry, and this was sufficient to condemn it in his eyes. His philosophical preference for freedom did not avail to overcome his repugnance to the persons and parties identified with its cause;

[1] Ch. xl. (*Hist.* v. p. 183).

while it permitted him to look with great placidity on the usurpations, tyrannies, and persecutions of the rulers who sought to crush it, and to find palliations and excuses for their worst acts.

The general course of the publication of the *History*, and the character of the reception it met with from the public, have been described in a previous chapter. The first volume, published in 1754, narrates, as was seen, the struggle for civil and religious liberty, from the accession of James up to the execution of Charles I. Here, most of all, the critics found reason to complain of Hume's strong spirit of partisanship, his unjustifiable bias, and his general untrustworthiness as an authority. In this volume his Tory leanings are extreme. He admits in numerous passages that liberty was being justly contended for, and maintains a certain appearance of partiality by blaming particular acts of James or Charles, or their instruments. But with little qualification he takes the side of the monarch, even in his most arbitrary exercises of power. He might be acting wrongly, but it is Hume's habitual contention that he had ancient or more recent precedents to justify him.[1] Whatever incidental concessions may be made, therefore, the scale, in nearly every instance of unconstitutional action, is caused to turn heavily against the opponents. It was not necessary that Hume should pretend—nor did he—that the Court of High Commission or the Star Chamber were salutary institutions; or that Hampden was not justified in his resistance to ship-money; or that Laud's

[1] *Hist.* vi. p. 52; cf. pp. 160 ff. The illusory character of many of these alleged precedents has been repeatedly shown (by Brodie, Hallam, and others).

character and policy were commendable; or that Charles acted wisely in his dealings with the Scots. But it was open to him to produce the same impression by subtler methods. When, for instance, the above-named engines of tyranny, the Court of High Commission and the Star Chamber, are represented as old and accredited instruments of justice,[1] and their victims are turned into ridicule as fanatics who got little more than they deserved;[2] when the King's arbitrary impositions are bolstered up by precedents,[3] and it is declared that "the grievances under which the English laboured," considered in themselves, "scarcely deserve the name";[4] when Hampden, notwithstanding his acknowledged virtues, is denied "the praises of a good citizen";[5] when Strafford is vindicated in his policy of "Thorough,"[6] and Laud is apologised for, his offences minimised, and his memory hallowed;[7] when the Covenanters are scoffed at for their fury against "the mild, the humane Charles, with his inoffensive liturgy,"[8] and their grievances are roundly declared to be "imaginary,"[9]—it is not easy to distinguish the result upon the mind from that of direct approval of the obnoxious measures. The Puritans are, of course, Hume's pet aversion, and the smallest possible allowance of respect is meted out to them.[10] They are seldom alluded to without some term of opprobrium being applied to them; their scruples about ceremonies are jeered at;[11] if they are called

[1] *Hist.* vi. pp. 160, 307, etc.
[2] *E.g.*, *ibid.* vi. pp. 295, 299.
[3] Cf. *ibid.* vi. p. 52.
[4] *Ibid.* vi. p. 319.
[5] *Ibid.* vi. p. 521.
[6] *Ibid.* vi. p. 418.
[7] *Ibid.* vii. p. 42.
[8] *Ibid.* vi. p. 330.
[9] *Ibid.* vi. p. 348.
[10] Cf. *ibid.* vi. pp. 11. 13, 85.
[11] *Ibid.* vii. pp. 13, 19, 203, 303.

to suffer for their opinions, it is well if a spice of mockery is not thrown into the description—always unsympathetic—of their sufferings.[1] They are gloomy, unreasonable, fanatical, hypocritical zealots; and while, in the character finally given of him, Charles, as man and ruler, is pictured as a model of all the virtues,[2] Cromwell, as we saw, is branded on his first appearance as "this fanatical hypocrite."[3]

It is scarcely to be wondered at that, as Hume tells us, this first volume was assailed on its appearance by a universal cry of disapprobation. The second volume, issued in 1756, covered the period from the death of Charles I. till the Revolution. It was, as before shown, better received. There was probably less room for the intrusion of the historian's offensive sentiments in this period; but it will be difficult entirely to exculpate Hume from deliberately toning down his work, and bating his breath, to secure for his book a more favourable reception. In this volume, too, a long note was inserted for the express purpose of explaining away the more violent and offensive statements in Vol. i. This was subsequently cancelled, and numerous alterations were made in later editions, all on the Tory side. Then, in 1759, appeared the third and fourth volumes, comprising the history of the House of Tudor. Portions of these volumes, especially in the reign of Elizabeth, contain some remarkably strong historical writing; but it is universally conceded that his desire to justify the actions of Charles I. led him, in this earlier period, to represent the Royal prerogative under the Tudors as much greater and more absolute than

[1] Cf. as above, vi. pp. 295, 299, etc.
[2] *Hist.* vii. p. 150.
[3] *Ibid.* vi. p. 274.

the facts will warrant. He had committed himself to an indefensible thesis, and was obviously shackled throughout. After this the work became more a matter of drudgery and profit than of inclination. What interest had the philosophical historian in "skirmishes of kites or crows,"[1] or in the doings and institutions of a people only emerging out of barbarism? Apart from the pleasingness of the style, therefore, Hume's account of the Anglo-Saxon and succeeding early periods presents little that is of permanent value to the student.

It is hardly necessary to speak of the influence which, as historian, Hume has exerted on our literature. For long his *History* was the standard book on the periods of which it treats. It entered largely into school instruction, and in this and more direct ways helped to form opinions and establish prejudices which in some instances have lasted to our own generation. Expurgated editions of it were produced for the use of "Christians."[2] Hosts of replies were published on the appearance of the several volumes, controverting what were thought to be their main misrepresentations. Most of its important errors have been pointed out by critics and historians since Hume's day—by none more fairly than by Mr. Hallam. But the *History* of Hume stills stands alongside of those of his con-

[1] *Hist.* i. p. 28.

[2] One such, published in 1816, bears the title—"Hume's History of England, Revised for Family Use, with such Omissions and Alterations as may render it Salutary to the Young, and unexceptionable to the Christian. Dedicated by Permission to the Right Rev. the Lord Bishop of Rochester, By the Rev. George Berkeley Mitchell, A.M., Vicar of St. Mary, in Leicester, etc. In Eight Vols." [The Alterations have only reference to the Church of England.]

temporaries Robertson and Gibbon as a great work of genius; and probably no historian of England will ever think himself properly equipped for his work till he has made himself familiar with its page and mastered the secret of its charm.

Our sketch may here close. No formal summing-up of the character and abilities of Hume is necessary after what has been said in the course of the foregoing narrative, exposition, and comment. Enough if it has been established that, for good or harm, Hume's memory and influence are likely to abide with us as long as our literature lasts.

APPENDIX

ON SOME EDITIONS OF HUME'S WORKS

[This Appendix is based partly on examination of the editions themselves, partly on the lists of editions in Hume's Works (A. & C. Black), vol. i., and in Green and Grose, vol. iii. pp. 85–6, with Mr. Grose's *History of Editions*. These are checked by reference to Burton, etc.]

The Philosophical Works

The Treatise of Human Nature, Being an Attempt to introduce the experimental Method of Reasoning into Moral Subjects. Book I. Of the Understanding. Book II. Of the Passions. London, John Noon[e], 1739 (two vols.).

Do. Book III. Of Morals. With an Appendix wherein some Passages of the foregoing volumes are illustrated and explained. London, Thomas Longman, 1740.

The above were recast and popularised as under:—

Philosophical Essays concerning Human Understanding. By the Author of the Essays, Moral and Political. London, A. Millar (April), 1748. (Includes Essays on Miracles and on A Particular Providence and a Future State.)

Do. Reprinted in November with the Author's Name (Grose, iii. pp. 48–9).

Do. Second edition, with Additions and Corrections.

London, A. Millar, 1750. [Publication delayed "because of the earthquakes," cf. Burton, i. p. 300.] Burton says it was published by Millar in 1751. Grose omits this edition (given in list in Black's vol. i.) and substitutes next.

Do. Second edition, with Additions and Corrections. London, M. Cooper. [Thus Grose. Copy in Bodl. Same edition transferred ?]

In the collected Essays (1758) the title of this work was changed to *An Enquiry concerning the Human Understanding*, by which it is generally known.

An Enquiry concerning the Principles of Morals. By David Hume, Esq. London, A. Millar, 1751.

The above, with the other Essays of Hume, were finally published under the general title of *Essays and Treatises on several Subjects* (1753–4, 1758, etc. See below).

The Essays and Dissertations

The history of the editions of the Essays is intricate, but the main facts are these. We take in order the *Essays Moral and Political*, the *Political Discourses*, and the *Four Dissertations*.

1. *Essays Moral and Political.* Edinburgh, A. Kincaid, 1741.

Do. Second edition, corrected, 1742.

Do. Vol. ii., 1742.

Do. Third edition (one vol.), corrected, with Additions. London, A. Millar; and Edinburgh, A. Kincaid, 1748.

As originally published, vol. i. of this collection contained 15 Essays, and vol. ii. 12 Essays,—27 in all, as compared with the 23 that appear in Part I. of the *Essays and Treatises*, in their final adjustment. The changes are accounted for as follows: (1) As many as 8 of the original Essays were gradually dropped, or were never reprinted, reducing the number to 19. Thus, the Essays on Essay-Writing, on Moral

Prejudices, and on the Middle Station in Life (in vol. ii.) were never reprinted. Other three (in vol. i.), on Impudence and Modesty, Love and Marriage, and the Study of History, were dropped in 1764. The Essay on Avarice (vol. i.) was dropped in 1770. Finally, the Essay on the Character of Sir Robert Walpole (vol. ii.) was first reduced to a footnote in 1748, and was finally omitted in 1770. (2) To balance these losses, three new Essays were added in 1748 (third edition), viz., those on the Original Contract, on Passive Obedience, and on National Characters [at first these were published separately]. The two former, however, were subsequently transferred to the *Political Discourses*, so that the gain thus far is only one Essay. (3) The Essay on the Origin of Government first appeared in the posthumous edition of 1777. (4) It will be seen below that two of the pieces originally published as *Dissertations*, viz., those on Tragedy and on The Standard of Taste, were in 1758 incorporated in Part I. of the "Essays, Moral, Political, and Literary." This total addition of 4 Essays brings up the number from 19 to the existing 23.

2. *Political Discourses.* By David Hume, Esq. Edinburgh, A. Kincaid and A. Donaldson, 1752. [Misprint in Grose of "*Gent. Mag.* Feb. 1742" for 1752.]

The volume as published in 1752 contained only 12 Essays as compared with the final 16. None were omitted (though title of second Essay is changed from "Luxury" to "Refinement in the Arts"); but it has been seen that two Essays (on Original Contract and Passive Obedience) were transferred to the group from the Moral and Political Essays, and two others were added in 1758, those, viz., on Jealousy of Trade and on Coalition of Parties. Thus the number 16 is made up.

Before referring to the final distribution, it is necessary to look to the complicated history of the *Four Dissertations.*

3. *Four Dissertations.* I. The Natural History of Religion. II. Of the Passions. III. Of Tragedy. IV. Of the Standard

of Taste. By David Hume, Esq. London, A. Millar, 1757.

In 1758 a readjustment was made in the *Essays and Treatises.* The Dissertation on the Passions (answering to Book II. of the *Treatise*, was appended to the *Enquiry concerning Human Understanding;* and the Natural History of Religion was similarly made to follow the *Enquiry concerning the Principles of Morals.* The two remaining Dissertations, those, viz., on Tragedy and on the Standard of Taste, were transferred to Part II. of the "Essays, Moral, Political, and Literary."

But besides this public history, the *Dissertations* had a secret history, which was only gradually unravelled. Originally it was meant to be a work of *Five* Dissertations, including two which were subsequently suppressed, namely, those on Suicide and on the Immortality of the Soul. [The Essay on the Standard of Taste was not yet inserted.] The Advocates' Library contains a first proof of the work, without title-page, but with the following in what is thought to be Hume's handwriting:—

Five Dissertations, to wit, The Natural History of Religion; of the Passions; of Tragedy; of Suicide; of the Immortality of the Soul. The Essay on Suicide is cut out in this copy, but that on Immortality remains.

It was vaguely known that suppression had taken place, but the facts were first brought clearly to light by the publication in 1784 of a book entitled "*Essays on Suicide and the Immortality of the Soul*, ascribed to the late David Hume, Esq. Never before published. With remarks, intended as an Antidote to the Poison contained in these Performances, by the Editor." The whole circumstances of the publication may be read in Burton or in Grose. It appears that Hume had at first intended to include as No. 1 of his list a Dissertation on Geometry. This was never printed. When the obnoxious Essays were suppressed, the Essay on the Standard of Taste was inserted to make up the volume.

It remains to refer to the final arrangement in the *Essays and Treatises.* First came—

Essays and Treatises on several Subjects. By David Hume, Esq.; in four volumes. London, A. Millar; Edinburgh, A. Kincaid and A. Donaldson, 1753–4.

The *Dissertations* intervened in 1757; then appeared—

Do. A New Edition, 1758 (one volume). To this edition is prefixed the following Advertisement: "Some alterations are made on the Titles of the Treatises, contained in the following volume. What in former editions was called *Essays Moral and Political*, is here entitled, Essays, Moral, Political, and Literary, Part I. The *Political Discourses* form the Second Part. What in former editions was called *Philosophical Essays concerning Human Understanding*, is here entitled *An Enquiry concerning Human Understanding.* The *Four Dissertations* lately published are dispersed through different Parts of this Volume."

The slight modifications made in subsequent editions of the Essays by omissions and additions have already been referred to. The editions (1760, 1764, 1768, 1770—finally the authoritative edition in 1777) vary from two to four volumes; the two-volume form prevailing. In the 1777 edition a section of the *Enquiry concerning Morals* was transferred to the Appendix under the title, Of Self Love.

The History

The dates of the publication of the successive volumes are given in the text, and need not be repeated. The authoritative edition is that of 1777, since reproduced in various forms.

INDEX

BUDDHA AND BUDDHISM.

BY ARTHUR LILLIE.

'Mr. Lillie has succeeded in clearly and lucidly mapping out the main broad facts of this fascinating religion.'—*Oxford Review.*

'His book is a solid performance, showing much industry and scholarship, and his presentation of Buddha and his message of peace, charity, and universal benevolence is both discriminating and sympathetic, and deserves hearty welcome.'—*Indian Review.*

WILLIAM HERSCHEL AND HIS WORK.

BY JAMES SIME, M.A., F.R.S.E.

'This book is one of an excellent series of biographical studies. . . . Probably many will share our first impression that another life of William Herschel was scarcely needed; but any such impression is likely to be removed by a perusal of the work before us. . . . All students of astronomy must feel an abiding interest in his career, and most of them will find much fresh information respecting it in the work before us, in which the story of his life is told with great freshness and vigour.'—*Athenæum.*

'Nothing remains but to praise this full and accurate account of his life and work. We have no work in the country which supplies what this volume gives in full.'—*Critical Review.*

FRANCIS AND DOMINIC AND THE MENDICANT ORDERS.

BY PROFESSOR JOHN HERKLESS, D.D.

'A scholarly and trustworthy sketch of the rise and progress of the Spanish and Italian Orders. . . . This volume is a worthy companion to Principal Lindsay's on "Luther"; and this is surely the highest praise we can give it.'—*Sword and Trowel.*

'Dr. Herkless gives a vivid picture of the progress of the two Orders, Franciscans and Dominicans, and also an even more striking account of their degradation.'—*Saint Andrew.*

SAVONAROLA.

BY REV. G. M'HARDY, D.D.

'A clear and plain account of the great Italian Reformer, written in a spirit of discriminating appreciation.'—*Christian World.*

'Dr. M'Hardy is fair, judicial, and yet considerate; his pages reveal the student, and he directs the reader to sources which will enable every one to frame a verdict on the sentence. . . . In this excellent work the substance, drift, and final meaning of this heroic yet visionary life are given.'—*Bookman.*

ANSELM AND HIS WORK.

BY REV. A. C. WELCH, B.D.

'Of distinct value and of first-rate interest. . . . There is not another book in our tongue that so admirably deals with a great man who left a deep mark both in the thought and policy of his time.'—*Methodist Times.*

'An admirable sketch quite worthy of companionship with the best volumes in this series of "The World's Epoch-Makers." It is learned, fair, sympathetic, and gives a vivid picture of the great statesman-divine. . . . We recommend its purchase and study to all who would learn the history of early religion in England.'—*Sword and Trowel.*

MUHAMMAD AND HIS POWER.

BY P. DE LACY JOHNSTONE, M.A.

'Every page of his brilliant, confident narrative reveals the man who knows.'—*Expository Times.*

'Gives in a moderate compass a thoroughly good popular account of Muhammad's career and influence.'—*Guardian.*

ORIGEN AND GREEK PATRISTIC THEOLOGY.

BY REV. W. FAIRWEATHER, M.A.

'A very interesting and scholarly monograph. The treatment is singularly complete. . . . Of real value. It is lucid in style, clear in its arrangement, and, while written by a sympathetic hand, gives an impression of perfect fairness of mind and trained historical sense.'

THE MEDICI AND THE ITALIAN RENAISSANCE.

BY OLIPHANT SMEATON, M.A.

'Their history is delightfully set forth in Mr. Smeaton's charming pages, which give evidence of wide and careful reading, masterly historical analysis, discriminating judgment, and sympathetic handling.'—*Aberdeen Journal.*

PLATO.

BY PROFESSOR D. G. RITCHIE, M.A., LL.D.

'The reader of this lucid volume will find that he is in the hands of a teacher who knows how to arouse and hold attention.'—*London Quarterly Review.*

[*Continued on next page.*

PRESS NOTICES—*Continued.*

"As a statement of the difficulties with which scepticism is confronted, nothing could be more excellent than the argument of this volume—an argument which is elaborated with an incisiveness and force that leave little to be desired. Many pages in the book are worth reading simply as a study in style."—*Baptist Magazine.*

"The work is no doubt by far the best exposition and defence of Christian claims that has been made in recent times. Differing as I am bound to do from most of the author's conclusions, I the more readily admit the ability and the apt method he has displayed in dealing with his subject."—Mr. CHARLES WATTS in *The Miracles of Christian Belief* (published by way of reply).

"It is written by an expert in science as well as theology, a fair-minded man who faces religious difficulties, not ignores them, and one who knows how to reason out his case like an accomplished advocate, without pressing it like an unscrupulous one. Mr. Ballard has rendered valuable service to the cause of Christian truth, and given us an excellent and useful book, deserving a large circulation."—*Methodist Recorder* (Prof. W. T. DAVISON, M.A., D.D.).

"The three defences of Christianity mentioned below have this in common, that they are worthy of the cause, original, sincere, convincing. Mr. Ballard is a controversialist, but a well-informed and generous one. He has been at pains not only to study the statements of unbelieving critics, but to understand the state of mind out of which they spring, and to see the sceptical position from the inside. He frankly acknowledges the sincerity and morality of much of the existing doubt, and in the conduct of his argument, although it is vigorous and unsparing, good feeling and good temper are conspicuous. . . . This argument, developed with Mr. Ballard's skill and force, is calculated to be of great service."—*British Weekly* (Prof. MARCUS DODS, D.D.).

"The science of Apologetics is not d[illegible] The hope of a better day wakens with the reading of a new book by Mr. Ballard. It is a full introduction to the modern science of Apologetics. The new ground is carefully chosen. In face of an enemy as hostile as ever, the opposition is uncompromising, but the warfare is less barbarous than of old. Even in the timely discussion of Haeckel's 'Riddle of the Universe' there is courtesy mingled with the vigour of the refutation."—*Expository Times.*

SPECIAL NOTICE.

By special request, Messrs. Clark are issuing the Eighth Chapter of this volume, entitled *"JESUS CHRIST: His Origin and Character,"* in separate form, with Cover. It is believed [illegible] at such an answer to the great central question: "What [illegible]k ye of Christ?" may, in these days, prove helpful to m[illegible] who not only recoil from Materialism or Secularism, b[illegible] equally unable to rest in the suggestions of what i[illegible]led "natural Christianity."

At the same [illegible] it is h[illegible]ed that this may lead to consideration o[illegible] [illegible]hole c[illegible] for Christian belief as set forth in the w[illegible] e men[illegible]ed.

The pric[illegible] XPE[illegible]" (by post, 7d.).

EDINBURGH: T. & T. CLARK, 38 GEORGE STREET.
NEW YORK: CHARLES SCRIBNER'S SONS.